ESEA — CHAPTER 2

[★]

PANAMA AND
THE UNITED STATES

[EDWARD F. DOLAN]

PANAMA
AND THE
UNITED STATES

THEIR CANAL,
THEIR STORMY YEARS

Franklin Watts ★ 1990
New York ★ London ★ Toronto ★ Sydney

Maps by Vantage Art

Photographs courtesy of: Photo Researchers: pp. 2 (Kantor), 21 (Frank),
76 (Randell), 97 (Latham), 123 (Goode); AP/Wide World: pp. 13, 129, 139,
143; Bettmann Archive: pp. 34, 49, 58, 66, 70, 86, 89, 93, 110; Brown
Brothers: pp. 38, 42, 57, 80, 82, 84, 88, 92; UPI/Bettmann News photos:
pp. 118; Magnum Photos: p. 133 (Meiselas)

Library of Congress Cataloging-in-Publication Data

Dolan, Edward F., 1924–
Panama and the United States: their canal, their stormy years /
by Edward F. Dolan.
p.   cm.
Includes bibliographical references.
Summary: A history of Panama's relations with the United States,
discussing how the construction of the Panama Canal caused years of
strife between the two nations and steps taken to improve relations.
ISBN 0-531-10911-9
1. United States—Foreign relations—Panama—Juvenile literature.
2. Panama—Foreign relations—United States—Juvenile literature.
3. Panama Canal (Panama)—History—Juvenile literature. [1. United
States—Foreign relations—Panama.   2. Panama—Foreign relations—
United States.   3. Panama Canal (Panama)—History.]   I. Title.
E183.8.P2D65   1990
327.7307287—dc20   89-24762   CIP   AC

CONTENTS

★ Also by Edward F. Dolan ★

America After Vietnam:
Legacies of a Hated War
Animal Rights
Anti-Semitism
Child Abuse
Cuba and the United States:
Troubled Neighbors
Drought:
The Past, Present, and Future Enemy
Drugs in Sports
The Insanity Plea
MIA: Missing in Action:
A Vietnam Drama
The New Japan
The Police in American Society
Victory in Europe:
The Rise and Fall of Hitler's Germany

[★]

PANAMA AND
THE UNITED STATES

[1]
THE BRIDGE OF LAND

The four ships raised sail on May 9, 1502. They moved slowly out of the Spanish port of Cadiz and gathered speed as they plunged into the Atlantic Ocean. They were tiny, narrow-hulled vessels called *caravels*. Crowded aboard them were one hundred fifty men, plus the supplies needed for a long and dangerous expedition. The expedition was commanded by Christopher Columbus.

THE FOURTH VOYAGE

Columbus was among the first navigators and geographers in history to hold a new view of the world. He believed the world was a globe and not the vast, flat expanse that everyone had always thought it to be. Because of this belief, he felt certain that, if he sailed west for a long enough time, he would finally drop anchor in an Asian port. It was the great dream of his life to do so.

This was now the Italian-born explorer's fourth voyage in search of a sea route across the Atlantic to the riches of the faraway Orient.

His earlier three voyages had been financed by the Spanish government.[1] Made in 1492, 1493, and 1498, they had taken Columbus clear across the Atlantic and into the great body of water that came to be called the Caribbean Sea.* There, he had ventured upon a number of islands. Among them were Cuba, Jamaica, and Puerto Rico. Columbus was delighted, for he was sure these islands lay just off the coast of the Orient. Instead he found that long miles of empty sea stretched westward from their shores. Without the supplies to travel on, Columbus returned home to Spain from the voyages in defeat.

Now he was back for another try. Columbus knew this might be the last chance to realize his great dream. Although only in his early fifties, he was a very sick man who looked far older than his years. His body was thin and wracked with gout and arthritis. He suffered from malaria, which he had contracted on one of his earlier trips. His face was drawn and pale and his once red hair was turning white. The hardships of three long voyages in small, wave-tossed ships had taken an awful toll on his health.

The explorer's health had also suffered from the stress of his dealings with Spain. The Spanish government had hoped to open a fine sea trade with the Orient via the route he promised to find. But, so far, Columbus had failed to keep his promise. The government was losing faith in him and his dream. It was only after he had long argued and pleaded that Spain had agreed to finance this new voyage.

Across the Caribbean

Nudged along by friendly winds, the caravels entered the Caribbean Sea in June.[2] Moving westward, they coasted

---

* The Caribbean Sea was named after the Caribe Indians, who inhabited its islands and the northern coast of South America.

Christopher Columbus

past the islands that the explorer had found earlier—islands that were now being settled by Spanish adventurers who collected Indian gold and farm crops to ship back home. Though his progress in July was stalled by a fierce hurricane, Columbus managed to put the islands far astern by month's end. It was then that he came upon a green land. It stretched across his westward path for as far as the eye could see in either direction.

The land did not loom just to the west. To the south, it swung about and thrust its way eastward back into the Caribbean. Columbus sailed down to the southern coast, dropped anchor, and went ashore. Hours later, he met an old Indian and heard some news that lifted his spirits. The Indian pointed eastward along the shore and spoke rapidly. Columbus had learned enough of the native Caribbean tongues on his earlier voyages to understand the man. He was saying that a rich kingdom lay off in that direction.

Columbus was sure the Indian was talking about the Orient. This caused the explorer to think that he had come to a giant cape near his long dreamed-of goal. If he sailed eastward, he thought, he would soon come to the end of the cape. He would curve around it and head west again for a short distance, and then surely mark the close of his great search.

The Long Coastline

Did the Indian actually know of a rich kingdom far off in the distance? Or was the old man simply trying to get rid of a feared stranger by saying that things were better somewhere else? No one knows. All that can be said is that the explorer quickly hoisted anchor and followed the shore eastward for a month. Then it turned south.

Columbus now felt his spirits plunge. He looked southward and saw the land stretch away mile after mile.

He had not come to the end of his "giant cape." Nowhere in sight was the Orient.

Columbus now had no choice but to travel down the coastline, no matter where it took him. As the days turned into weeks, the caravels inched their way past shores that were sometimes rocky and sometimes choked with jungle growth. In November, the land again began to swing eastward. Columbus followed the swing and finally anchored in a bay that would become known as Nombre de Dios Bay (meaning "Name of God"). Here, his search for the foot of his "giant cape" came to an end.

Columbus knew that he could sail no farther. His supplies were running out. His remaining foodstuffs were rotting. His men had been away from home for seven long months. They were exhausted and close to starving. The men felt that Columbus would never find his water passage to the Orient. They wanted to go home—now. He was in danger of a mutiny at any moment.

The Settlement at Belen

Bitterly disappointed, the explorer turned back along the coast and headed for the mouth of a river he had visited some days earlier. There, he had been greeted by Indians who wore jewelry made of gold. He now planned to trade blankets, mirrors, and trinkets for the gold. The Spanish government would be delighted when he returned with such a treasure, even though he had failed again to discover a sea route to the rich Orient.

The ships reached the mouth of the river in January 1503. The river is known today as the Chagres. Columbus and his men went ashore and christened the spot Belen ("Bethlehem") in honor of Epiphany Sunday, the day of their landing. They built several small huts, made friends with the surrounding Indians, and got down to the work of trading baubles, cooking gear, and blankets for gold.

Slowly over the next few months, the ships began to fill with treasure. But then things went wrong. Trouble erupted between the natives and the visitors. Each side attacked the other. Finally, after one especially vicious Indian assault, Columbus fled Belen and headed home with his men, never again to return to this jungle shore, and never again to search for his sea route to the Orient. After a year's stop at Jamaica, the explorer arrived in Spain in 1504. He died two years later.

THE BRIDGE OF LAND

Columbus, of course, was correct in his view of the world as a globe. But he was dead wrong when he thought that his Caribbean voyage had brought him to a giant cape. The land along which he had traveled to Nombre de Dios Bay and the Chagres River was not a cape on the outskirts of the Orient. Rather, it was a giant natural land bridge that spanned the distance between the North and South American continents.

The bridge marked the end of what was already known in the explorer's day as the New World. Later, voyagers would follow the vast Pacific Ocean to its opposite side. Far across the Pacific, thousands of miles from where Columbus thought it to be, lay the Orient.

The land where Columbus came upon Nombre de Dios Bay and the Chagres River ranges today along the Caribbean coast of the Republica de Panama (Republic of Panama).3 The name *Panama* comes from an old Indian word meaning "a place where many fishes are taken." The nation's people are called Panamanians.

Originally the home of many Indian tribes, Panama served as a Spanish possession from the time of Columbus to the early 1800s. It then became a part of the South American nation, Colombia, and remained a Colombian holding until winning its independence with the help of the United States in 1903. Today, Panama is the southernmost of the seven nations that occupy the bridge of land. Its fellow countries are Belize, * Guatemala, Honduras (where Columbus met the old Indian), El Salvador, Nicaragua, and Costa Rica. Together, they make up the area known as Central America. Lying at the northern end of the bridge is Mexico. It is not considered a part of Central America.

After falling southward for long miles, the bridge of land, as Columbus learned, curved eastward. Panama, which looks something like an S that has toppled forward on its face, stretches along this curve. Consequently, for much of its length, it runs in the same direction as the United States—from west to east. Just before reaching the South American mainland, it dips south again. On its western border lies Costa Rica. At its South American border, it joins Colombia.

PANAMA

Panama is an *isthmus* country, so called because it is a narrow strip of land with water on either side.[4] It occupies what is formally called the Isthmus of Panama. On its northern side, the Caribbean Sea stretches off to the Atlantic Ocean. On the southern side is the Pacific Ocean. The Caribbean coastline runs for 477 miles (768 km), and the Pacific shore for 767 miles (1,234 km). The land in between ranges in width from 30 (48 km) to 120 (193 km) miles. Altogether, Panama covers 29,209 square

---

* Belize is the newest of the Central American nations. It was once a British possession and was known as British Honduras. It has been an independent nation since 1981.

THE CARIBBEAN AND CENTRAL & SOUTH AMERICA

UNITED STATES

Gulf of Mexico

MEXICO

CUBA

HAITI

DOMINICAN REP.

BELIZE

JAMAICA

GUATEMALA HONDURAS *Caribbean Sea*

EL SALVADOR NICARAGUA

COSTA RICA

PANAMA

VENEZUELA GUYANA

SURINAM

FRENCH GUIANA

COLOMBIA

ECUADOR

PERU

BRAZIL

BOLIVIA

PARAGUAY

A T L A N T I C   O C E A N

P A C I F I C   O C E A N

URUGUAY

ARGENTINA

CHILE

miles (75,800 sq km), making it almost exactly half the size of the state of Michigan.

A chain of mountains and hills splits Panama lengthwise. The mountains show their highest peaks at either end of the country, with the tallest of their number rising to just over 11,000 feet (3,353 m). They sink to their lowest altitudes at the nation's midpoint; there, some manage heights of just a few hundred feet. The whole chain is covered with jungle and semi-deciduous forests, and is pockmarked with valleys and plains.

A Tropical Land

Panama is a tropical country. The climate is rainy and humid. The rain is heaviest on the Caribbean side, where it can total 128 inches (325 cm) a year, or unleash as much as 155 inches (394 cm). On the Pacific side, the rain averages less than 70 inches (178 cm) annually. The Pacific side is blessed with a dry season that runs from December through April. The Caribbean side also has a dry season, but it is much shorter.

The nation, however, enjoys an atmospheric temperature that is kinder than those found in other tropical regions. It averages 80° F (25° C) year round.

The People of Panama

Today Panama is the home of slightly more than 2 million people. They represent a variety of ethnic groups, the main one being the mestizo, which accounts for about 70 percent of the population. The term *mestizo* originally referred to people of mixed Spanish-Indian blood. It is applied today to persons of any racial mixture. Caucasians make up 10 percent of the population; West Indians, 14 percent; and Indians, 6 percent. The principal languages are, first, Spanish and then, English. Also spoken in the rural areas are a number of Indian tongues.

It is estimated that, at the time Columbus arrived, there were about sixty Indian tribes living in Panama. Some historians have set the number of their people at a half-million. Others disagree with this figure and claim that one major tribe alone—the Cuna—accounted for 750,000 people. The native population was drastically reduced by the diseases introduced by the early Spanish settlers, and by the harsh treatment shown the Indians by the newcomers.

Panama at Work

Though Panama has several large and modern cities—chief among them Colón on the Caribbean side and Panama City (the national capital) on the Pacific coast—it is principally a country of small towns and farms. Close to a third of the Panamanian people are employed in farming. On tracts of land usually no more than 25 acres (10.12 ha) each, they raise bananas, rice, corn, beans, pineapples, sugar, cacao, coffee, and coconuts. Farm crops are Panama's chief exports. Bananas, sugar, and coffee top the list of commodities shipped to foreign lands. Also exported, as can be gleaned from the Indian word that gave the country its name, are such sea "crops" as fish meal and shrimp.

Since most of Panama is covered with dense forests and jungles, only about 25 percent of the land has been cultivated. As a result, since farm produce must be exported to help the national economy, what remains of the nation's crops is not sufficient to feed the entire population, and Panama must import most of its food. The same situation exists for industrial raw materials and manufactured goods such as automobiles, machinery, and clothing. Because Panama must import more than it is able to export it is not a wealthy country. It is deeply in debt. The Panamanian debt to foreign nations currently stands at over $4 billion, one of the highest in all Latin America.

Laborers load a chief Panama export—bananas —onto a shipping dock in Panama City.

In addition to its agricultural activities, Panama refines oil for export and for domestic use. It is also one of the centers of world banking. And it boasts one of the world's largest merchant fleets. This is because many foreign nations register their ships with Panama to take advantage of the nation's low registry fees. Some eleven thousand ships have Panamanian registry.

THE GREAT CANAL

In international trade, Panama ranks as one of the world's most important countries. Its importance stems from the fact that it is a narrow isthmus—a land so slender that it separates the Pacific and Atlantic oceans by a mere 30 miles (48 km) at one point. (The Caribbean Sea is considered to be an arm of the Atlantic.) For centuries, the trading nations of the world saw that the country's narrowness made it an ideal place to link the two oceans by means of a man-made waterway—a canal.[5] The canal, would prove a boon to all the ships that traveled back and forth between the Atlantic and Pacific because it would save tremendous amounts of time and money.

The dreamed-of waterway—the Panama Canal— took shape early in this century. When it was opened in 1914, it did indeed prove a boon to international sea traffic. No longer did merchant vessels, passenger liners, and warships bound from the Atlantic to the Pacific, or vice versa, have to work their way down around the foot of South America. Saved were costly and at times dangerous journeys that, depending on a vessel's destination, covered distances of 10,000 miles (16,100 km) or more and took weeks to complete. The Canal cut the passage from one ocean to the other to a mere 40.27 miles (65 km) across the Isthmus, and the trip itself to a handful of hours— about nine in all. For example, a ship bound from New

York City to San Francisco travels 4,800 miles (7,728 km) if it crosses the Caribbean and passes through the Canal. But, were it to sail down and around South America, it would travel 12,600 miles (20,290 km) before reaching San Francisco. Saved are 7,800 miles (12,560 km)—and the extra costs of running the ship.

The Panama Canal stands as a magnificent achievement in engineering history. On the Atlantic (Caribbean) side, the Canal begins at the city of Colón and slices across man-made lakes, through jungles and low hills, to Panama City on the Pacific. Many people mistakenly think that the Canal runs from east to west. Because Panama itself extends from east to west, the Canal actually traces a path from north to south, specifically from northwest to southeast.

Built and until recently controlled by the United States, the Canal has done more than just link two of the world's great oceans. It has strongly affected the Panamanian economy. The United States has long paid Panama an annual fee from the tolls charged ships for using the Canal. Today, that payment ranges up to $80 million a year. Further, the Canal has been a major source of local employment. Over the years, thousands of Panamanians have been employed in its daily operation. Thousands more have profited from selling goods and services to Canal operators, passing ships, and to the United States military forces stationed along the waterway for its defense.

A Troubled Linkage

In yet another way, the Canal has done far more than just connect the Atlantic and Pacific. It has linked the histories of Panama and the United States from the very day at the dawn of this century when the United States government decided to build the waterway. That linkage has proven to be a troubled one. Despite the Canal's economic advantages, many Panamanians have long complained of its presence in their midst. They objected, for instance, to having a foreign-controlled waterway splitting their country in half. They angrily contended that the Canal made it easy for the United States to interfere in their nation's affairs. They claimed that the Canal produced a Panama that was not an independent nation but a mere possession of the U.S. These complaints—and other factors that we'll discuss later—led to an agreement in 1977 that will see America relinquish control of the Canal by the end of the century.

★ ★ ★

In all, the Canal has given the United States and Panama a stormy twentieth century. In this book, we're going to see:

> How the magnificent dream of an Atlantic-Pacific link first took shape;
>
> How the magnificent dream finally became an even more magnificent reality;
>
> How Panama, because of the waterway, won its independence from Colombia with American help;
>
> How the Panama Canal then caused years of strife between the new nation and its giant neighbor far to the north;
>
> And how, because all of all the strife, the Canal will soon pass out of American hands.

For a complete view of all that has occurred, we must go back in time to the 1500s. It was then, beginning with the exploits of a handsome Spanish adventurer, that the Canal story began.

THE MAGNIFICENT DREAM

Columbus was not the first European to reach the shores of Panama.

In 1501, a year before the explorer set sail on his fourth voyage, another explorer entered the Caribbean. He was Rodrigo de Bastidas of Spain, a wealthy business-man. Commanding an expedition of two ships, he nosed along the northern coast of South America. He was look-ing for gold and his quest carried him as far west as Nombre de Dios Bay before he returned home. [1]

Bastidas earned a place in history by becoming the first European to cruise along the Panama coastline. But a far greater place was won by a member of his expedition— a young, fair-haired Spanish adventurer named Vasco Núñez de Balboa.

BALBOA

Practically nothing is known of Balboa's early life, other than that he was born around 1475. [2] He was about 26 years old when he sailed with the Bastidas expedition.

While en route home to Spain at the close of that voyage, Bastidas stopped at the island of Hispaniola (now the site of Haiti and the Dominican Republic), where a thriving Spanish settlement was taking shape. Balboa obviously liked what he saw there, for he left the ship, made the island his home, and started a small farm. He remained on Hispaniola for nine years.

By the end of that time, Balboa was in trouble with some of the islanders. Apparently, he was a carefree man who had no talent for business and who preferred having a good time to the arduous work of operating a farm. As a result, he had run up a great many debts over the years and had no idea how he was ever going to pay them off. And so he decided on a drastic action when he learned that two ships were being readied for a voyage out from Hispaniola. Commanded by a man named Martín Enciso, the ships were to carry supplies to a settlement that the explorer Alonso Ojeda had founded far along the South American coast. When Enciso ordered several casks of food from Balboa's farm, the young Spaniard suddenly saw a way to escape his debts and to have a fine adventure in the bargain. He climbed into one of the casks, pulled the lid into place above his head, and remained crouched there as his hiding place was swung aboard one of the vessels.

Once he was safely at sea, Balboa inched his way out of the cask and presented himself to a surprised Enciso. By then, it was too late to turn back to Hispaniola. Balboa was on his way to a great adventure—and to an honored place in the history of the New World.

THE DARIEN ADVENTURE

Enciso's ships sailed far west along the South American coast, passing the lands that are today the nations of Venezuela and Colombia. Their journey at last brought them to the Gulf of Darien, a broad waterway that pokes its way into Colombia. The Gulf is shaped so it runs roughly from north to south. The western side of its mouth lies close to what is now the border of Panama.

The ships ventured but a short distance into the Gulf before reaching Ojeda's settlement. But Enciso's men only found the settlement in ruins.

Starvation and Poisoned Arrows

It did not take long for Enciso to learn what had happened. Ojeda had landed several months before with three hundred men. Ojeda's purpose was to take the surrounding Indians prisoner, and send them home to Spain as slaves. The Indians, however, had no intention of being captured. When attacked, they fought back savagely with bows and arrows. Any man struck by the arrows died a horrible, pain-wracked death, for the arrow tips were coated with poison. Once the intruders had been repulsed, the Indians put the settlement under siege.

Slowly, over the next months, the Spaniards either died of the arrow poison or of starvation as their supplies ran out. Ojeda had sailed off some weeks before to seek help. Not wanting to abandon the settlement, he had left a number of men behind, promising to return as soon as possible with food and reinforcements. He was never heard from again. Of the three hundred men who had come to the Gulf settlement, only sixty remained.

Now, bolstered by Enciso's men and supplies, the survivors thought they could hang on until Ojeda returned. But the Indians increased their attacks. The new supplies dwindled away while poisoned arrows kept raining down on the Spaniards. With men dying every day, Enciso was at a loss. Should he sail off and perhaps be accused of cowardice for deserting a post that might one day supply Spain with slaves? Or should he wait for Ojeda to appear with reinforcements? If he waited, he would risk the loss of all his men, not to mention his own life.

It was at this point that Balboa stepped forward. He told Enciso of his voyage with Bastidas. He recalled how the expedition had come upon an Indian village surrounded by fine fields of grain. The Indians there were friendly. And there was gold to be found nearby. He was sure that the village lay somewhere just across the Gulf of Darien.

Enciso told Balboa to lead the way to this fine place. Under the young man's direction, the ships crossed the Gulf. Then, as Balboa had expected, a short sail along the Panamanian coast brought them to the village. This time the Spaniards were delighted to see the Indians flee in terror at the sight of the ships. The village, its food stores, and the surrounding grain fields were abandoned to the newcomers without a fight. Settling down to fill their bellies, the men gave the village a name, Santa Maria de la Antigua ("St. Mary of Antigua"), in honor of the Blessed Virgin.

As Balboa had said, there was much gold to be found nearby. Happily, the men began to collect it, certain that they were making themselves rich. Then trouble erupted. Enciso told the men that, contrary to the usual practice of Spanish expeditions, they could not keep a share of the gold for themselves. All the gold had to be sent back to Spain. Immediately, Enciso was faced with a rebellion. Again, Balboa stepped forward. This time, he took the command of the village away from Enciso.

Back on Hispaniola, Balboa had been a man who liked a good time more than hard work, but, here at Santa Maria, he proved to be something else. He revealed himself to be an excellent leader.

In Command at Santa Maria
Upon taking command, Balboa promised the men fair treatment in the distribution of the gold they found. The

men, liking and admiring him, ended their rebellion and acknowledged him as their new leader. An angry Enciso was sent home to Spain.

From then on, the settlement at Santa Maria flourished. In a matter of months, Balboa brought the surrounding countryside under his control. He did so by befriending the Indians and beginning a trade with them. In many ways, Balboa was far different from many other Spanish adventurers who were coming to the New World. They were hated and feared by the Indians for their cruelty. But Balboa—though he could be hard when necessary and though he enslaved many Indians—had the general reputation of dealing fairly and courteously with the tribes around him.

Word of Balboa's accomplishments made its way back to Spain. The king appointed him governor of Santa Maria and its surrounding area. More and more settlers began to appear on the Panama coast as the months passed. By 1513—just three years after his arrival—Balboa's territory had become one of the most successful of Spain's New World holdings.

That year, Balboa made a journey that was to give him a lasting place in history and thereupon begin the dream of a canal across the Isthmus. For as long as he had been in Panama, Balboa had heard the Indians speak of a great sea that lay on the opposite side of the land. The Indians said it was no more than a short but very dangerous journey away. And so, on September 1, 1513, Balboa set out to see this vast body of water for himself.

JOURNEY TO THE PACIFIC

Balboa began his journey with 190 Spanish companions and about a thousand Indians to carry the supplies.[3] To this day, no one is certain of where he started the trip or of

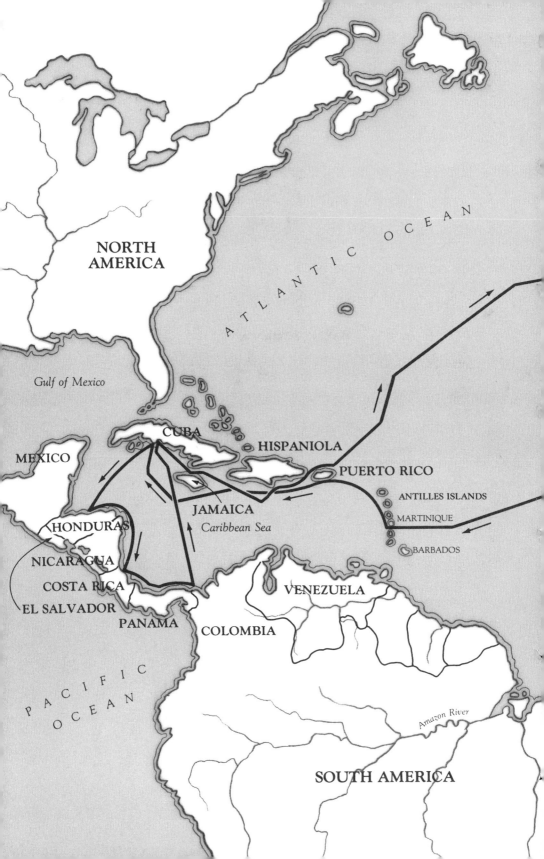

NORTH
AMERICA

ATLANTIC OCEAN

Gulf of Mexico

CUBA

HISPANIOLA

PUERTO RICO

MEXICO

ANTILLES ISLANDS

JAMAICA

Caribbean Sea

MARTINIQUE

HONDURAS

BARBADOS

NICARAGUA

COSTA RICA

VENEZUELA

EL SALVADOR

PANAMA

COLOMBIA

PACIFIC
OCEAN

Amazon River

SOUTH AMERICA

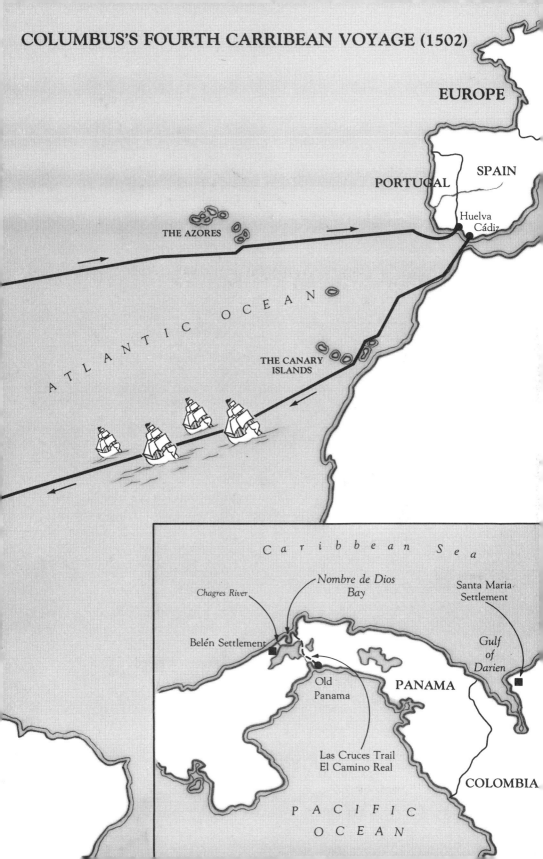

the actual route he took across the Isthmus. What is known, however, is that his men had to hack their way through dense jungles and hike over forested hills. It was a trek that soon proved hard on the Spaniards, no matter how tough they were.

Dressed in the heavy armor of sixteenth-century soldiers, some found every step an exhausting one, so drained were they of energy by the heat and humidity. Some men fell ill with dysentery after drinking the water they scooped up from streams and muddy pools along the way. Some suffered painful cuts as they pushed through the underbrush and were slashed by it. Because of these hardships, Balboa managed to cover only a scant few miles each day. He moved slowly so that the sick and injured could keep up with their fellow marchers. He stopped often to wait for stragglers.

Slowing his progress even more were the Indian tribes that lived along his path. Before he could pass through their lands, he had to stop and befriend them. On at least one occasion, he had to fight his way past a hostile tribe.

Altogether, the journey covered about 50 miles (80 km). But it took almost a month to complete. On September 26, 1513, Balboa climbed the final hill in his path. On reaching its crest, he stopped and caught his breath. Dead ahead, far in the distance, lay the vast sea that his Indian friends had described. Because Panama runs from east to west, Balboa was looking southward at the time. To the body of water he saw, Balboa gave the name "The Great South Sea." Later, explorers rechristened it the Pacific Ocean.

Balboa spent another four days hiking down to the water's edge. Clad in full armor, he marched into the surf, raised his sword high, and claimed the Great South Sea and all the shores it touched for the Spanish king.

Balboa takes possession of the Pacific in the name of the king and queen of the Castile.

PANAMA:
A SPANISH GEM

The Spanish settlement in Panama grew even more successful because of Balboa's discovery.[4] During the next years, Spanish explorers sailed down the Pacific coast of South America, eventually bringing such mineral-rich Indian nations as Peru, Bolivia, and Argentina under their control. As a result, Panama became more than an important holding; in one way, it became *the* most important of Spain's New World possessions.

Panama's location and narrowness made it ideal for the quick transportation of New World wealth back to Spain. Up the Pacific Ocean to Panama came an unending stream of ships carrying gold from Peru, silver from Bolivia, and pearls from the islands off the South American coast. Goods from the Spanish settlements along the Pacific coast of the Central American lands to the north of Panama also took the same route. Saved in all instances were long and dangerous journeys down around the foot of South America and thence across the Atlantic to Spain.

The ships made port at the blossoming settlement of Panama City (located a short distance from modern Panama City and now known as Old Panama). Their cargoes were unloaded and hauled by mule train across the Isthmus to Nombre de Dios Bay, where waiting galleons took them aboard for the trip to Spain.

El Camino Real

To speed up cross-country shipments, the Spanish put hordes of Indian laborers to the task of building a road from the Pacific to the Atlantic side of the Isthmus.[5] First called the Las Cruces Trail ("The Crossing Trail") and then El Camino Real ("The Royal Road"), the road began at Panama City and ran for a distance of about 40 miles

(64 km) to Nombre de Dios Bay. Though paved with stone, it was little more than a muddy track that, at its widest, measured just 8 feet (2.4 m) across. Later, a second trail was added. It branched away from the main road and ran along the Chagres River to the Caribbean.

The two trails, with the jungle underbrush constantly trying to spread back over them, gave the Spanish all sorts of trouble. There were delays when the mule trains became mired in the mud. And there were times of the year when the rains totally closed the roads, forcing cargoes worth millions to lie idle in warehouses at Panama City. These problems gave birth to an idea that promised to make the crossing easier and more dependable—the idea of a *canal* that would link the Pacific and the Atlantic oceans. The dream of what would eventually be one of the world's greatest engineering feats began to take shape.

And what of Balboa, whose discovery had made the thoughts of the waterway possible? He was dead by the time the dream took shape. Despite his fine work, the adventurer had earned many enemies back in Spain. All were friends of Enciso who hated Balboa for taking the leadership at Santa Maria away from him. They succeeded in having the king send a new governor out to Panama to replace Balboa. The new governor then falsely accused the explorer of treason and had him beheaded in 1517.[6]

THE DREAMERS

Three points must be made before continuing our story. First, the dream of where to build an Atlantic-Pacific canal was not limited to the site of Panama alone. Early on, a number of Spanish explorers suggested a variety of locations for such a waterway. Some, for example, felt that it could be cut across Mexico. Others said that the area which is now Nicaragua would serve quite as well.

Second, the early dreams of a water passage did not come from any one man. The idea was shared by many. And, finally, all those dreams came to nothing. [7]

The Portuguese Explorer
Among the earliest dreamers was a Portuguese explorer named Alvara de Saavedra. While exploring Central America in the 1520s, he visited several locations where he thought a canal could be built. One was an area that stretched across the waist of Panama and was quite near to the region through which the Panama Canal now passes. He told his companions of his plan to inform the king of Spain that a waterway 8 feet (2.4 m) wide could be cut there. Saavedra never had the chance to speak with the king, however. The explorer died before returning to Europe.

An Impossible Job
In 1534, King Charles I of Spain (also known as Holy Roman Emperor Charles V) showed his interest in a Panamanian waterway. Having no idea where it could be placed, he ordered the governor of Panama to make a survey of the Isthmus and then report on any routes that seemed possible. When the survey was completed, the governor had discouraging news. He reported that the construction of a canal was out of the question. No one could forge a path through the dense jungles and forests. And the tropical diseases found in Panama would surely kill off all the workers. It was widely known that these diseases had decimated the work crews who had laid down the Las Cruces Trail.

Because of the governor's report, Spanish interest in the construction of a canal waned for many years. But it was revived for a time in the late 1500s by King Philip II.

He sent a team of engineers from Spain to look for possible routes. They ended up being as pessimistic as the governor. For the very same reasons he had given, they held that a waterway across Panama was an engineering impossibility.

"God's Will"

King Philip responded by saying that no man would ever be able to build an Isthmian canal because it was "God's will" that it not be constructed. He announced that, if God had wanted a waterway across Panama, it would have been put there at the time of the Creation.

There was more than religious belief behind Philip's announcement. The British crown, wanting to get its hands on the New World riches being reaped by Spain, had been sending out privateers for years to attack and seize the treasure-laden ships leaving Nombre de Dios Bay. As a result, the attackers had brought home to England captured cargoes worth millions. They had also laid siege to a number of Spanish settlements on both the Pacific and Atlantic sides of the Isthmus. The successes recorded by the privateers led the Spanish king to fear that a waterway across the Isthmus would make it all the easier for future intruders to sail into Panama and gain a foothold there.

And so, not wanting to admit he was afraid, Philip decreed that God did not want the canal built. Then, to make sure that no Spanish adventurer ignored the decree, he said that anyone who tried to build a passage of any sort across the Isthmus would be arrested and put to death.

King Philip's announcement put an end to the earliest Spanish dreams of a canal. Interest in the waterway faded and was all but forgotten during the 1600s. The 1700s, however, produced a brief flurry of interest when Spain, after some 200 years, overturned Philip's edict and

King Philip II of Spain

again sent a commission to Nicaragua to locate a possible route there. The effort came to nothing. Again, Spanish interest waned.

Then the 1800s dawned. The interest suddenly sparked anew. This time, however, it was not confined to Spain. The idea appealed to a number of other countries as well, all of whom fully understood the value of an Atlantic-Pacific connection. Among them was the young country, the United States of America.

[3]

A NEW AND GROWING INTEREST

During the five years between 1799 and 1804, a young German naturalist explored vast reaches of Spain's New World holdings. It was this exploration that triggered the new—and what would be an ever growing—interest in an Atlantic-Pacific waterway.

The young man was Baron Alexander von Humboldt. [1] Born in 1769, Humboldt was only thirty years old at the time he began his trip, but he was already recognized as one of Europe's finest scientists. Before his death in 1859, he would be widely acclaimed as the second most famous European of the nineteenth century, surpassed only by Napoléon Bonaparte.

Accompanied by his close friend French botanist Aimé Bonpland, Humboldt launched his New World adventure with a canoe trip of some 1600 miles along Venezuela's Orinoco River. The journey proved what many geographers had long suspected—that the Orinoco is linked to the Amazon River. The connection is made by means of a vast watershed region deep in the jungle.

Alexander von Humboldt

Next, Humboldt traveled to Colombia and then hiked south through the Andes Mountains to Peru. He spent much of his time in Peru studying the deposits of *guano** (bird droppings) that littered the coast.

THE NINE ROUTES

For the purposes of our story, the most important part of Humboldt's journey came when he departed Peru and sailed north along the Pacific coast to Central America and Mexico (on this leg of the trip, he also studied the major Pacific current that now bears his name, the Humboldt Current). He stopped at Panama for a mule trip across the Isthmus via the remains of the old El Camino Real and then moved on to visit Guatemela, Honduras, and Mexico.

Why were these stops so important? They enabled Humboldt, on his return home, to write that he had found no fewer than nine Central American locations where an Atlantic-Pacific canal could be built. The best of the lot, he said, followed Panama's El Camino Real from Panama City to the mountains and thence along the branch that led down the Chagres River to the Caribbean coast.

In the years following his journey, Humboldt wrote a seemingly endless series of scientific books and articles. His works were widely read throughout Europe. But none triggered a greater interest than did his writings on the nine suggested canal routes. His words reminded every European nation of the many economic, military, and

* For centuries, the local Indians had used the substance *guano* as fertilizer. Humboldt sent sample droppings to France for study. They were found to be so rich in nitrate and phosphate that 1 ton (1.11 t) of guano could do the work of 33 tons (36.5 t) of ordinary fertilizer. The study of those samples led to the development of one of today's major agricultural industries.

political benefits that could come from an Atlantic-Pacific waterway.

Economically, it would save huge sums of money by enabling merchant ships to pass from ocean to ocean without that long sail down around the foot of South America. Militarily, it would permit a nation to send its warships and troops much more quickly to distant trouble spots.

And what of the nation that built and controlled the canal? What political power it would hold by being in the position to allow only its friends the use of the waterway! And what riches it would reap from the fees charged to ships traveling the passage!

The governments of Spain, France, Germany, Great Britain, and Holland, plus a number of private companies—all were suddenly interested in building and controlling the waterway. Spain, because of her vast Central and South American possessions, was the first to move. In 1814, she ordered that the waterway be cut along Humboldt's favorite route—the El Camino Real in Panama.

TROUBLES IN
THE NEW WORLD

But the work was never done because Spain was in trouble with its holdings in both South and Central America and was rapidly losing control over them. The area was now heavily populated by Spaniards who had been born in the New World. The New Worlders looked on the holdings not as Spanish possessions but as their own homelands. Tired of Spanish domination, they were in no mood to cooperate in the forging of a canal for the mother country. What they really wanted was to break free and become independent nations.[2]

As a result, a series of revolutionary movements began to take shape throughout South and Central America. Those movements not only put an end to Spain's plans for the canal but also broke its hold on the New World.

The South American
Freedom Movements

In South America, the movements were led by two military figures, Simon Bolívar and José de San Martín. Bolívar played a key role in liberating four holdings and turning them into four independent nations—Colombia in 1819, Venezuela in 1821, Peru in 1824, and Bolivia (named in his honor) in 1825. San Martín helped Argentina win its independence in 1816 and then marched an army across the Andes to wrest Chile from Spanish hands in 1817. He then joined Bolívar in the fight to free Peru.

For Panama, the liberation of Colombia was the most significant of all the bids for freedom. After the Isthmus had started life as a holding under Balboa, the Spanish government had first made it a part of Peru and then, in 1717, joined it with Colombia to form the province of Nueva Granada (New Spain). For two years after Colombia had won its independence,* the Spanish and their supporters continued to rule in Panama. But, on November 10, 1821, the Panamanians declared themselves free of Spain. Then, because of the commercial advantages promised by a union with Colombia, Panama elected to remain a part of that country. It stayed with Colombia until late in the century.

---

* Colombia, on winning its independence, established itself as the republic of New Granada. It continued to be known as New Granada until 1861 when, in honor of Christopher Columbus, it adopted its present name, the Republic of Colombia.

The Freedom Movements
North of Panama

The moves toward freedom from Spain were seen in the holdings north of Panama before they erupted in South America. Mexico had begun to challenge Spanish authority in 1810 and finally broke away in 1821. At that time, its five neighbors to the south—Guatemala, Honduras, El Salvador, Nicaragua, and Costa Rica—became part of the Mexican Empire.

The five, however, soon claimed their independence from Mexico and knit themselves together in what they called the Central American Federation. The Federation was marked throughout its brief history by strife among its member states. It finally disbanded in 1839, at which time the five members became independent nations.

And so, by the mid-1820s Spain had lost its power in the New World. All that was left were some of its Caribbean islands. Unable to build the waterway during the years of revolution, Spain once and for all ended its dream of forging an Atlantic-Pacific canal.

THE FEDERATION YEARS

The member states of the Central American Federation may have battled each other constantly, but they were all agreed on one point. They understood the myriad advantages that an Atlantic-Pacific waterway could bring them. They wanted it built somewhere in their area.

There were problems, however. They had neither the funds nor the technical expertise necessary to undertake such a massive project by themselves. They needed an outsider to build the canal for them.

Their first choice was the United States.[3] In the late 1820s, several Federation representatives traveled to Washington, D.C., for talks with Secretary of State Henry

Clay. Clay, after hearing the special advantages that would be granted to the United States for taking the job, expressed a deep interest in the project. But, for two reasons, nothing then came of the matter. First, the United States was devoting all its energies to its westward expansion. Second, the young country was not yet a wealthy nation. It did not have the time, money, or manpower to take on the job.

A short time later, one of the Federation states—Nicaragua—gave the rights to build a canal across its land to a French engineering firm. When the company found itself unable to handle the work, it transferred its rights to De Witt Clinton, the American political leader who had been a key figure in the building and completion in 1825 of the Erie Canal across New York's Hudson River and Lake Erie. The experienced Clinton was an excellent choice for the new project. But, again, all amounted to nothing when the company could not raise enough money for the job.

The Nicaraguans then turned to Holland and signed an agreement to have the Dutch build their canal. This time the whole matter was dropped when the United States objected to the plan.

The United States objection was based on the argument that the Nicaraguan-Dutch plan constituted a violation of the Monroe Doctrine.

THE MONROE DOCTRINE AND THE CANAL

The Monroe Doctrine was a United States government policy named for its creator, President James Monroe.4 He had announced the policy in a speech to Congress in late 1823. Remembering how such nations as Spain and England had exploited their New World holdings, and sharply aware that a number of European governments still had their eye on the New World, he told Congress that the countries of North, Central, and South America must never again be looked on as targets for foreign ownership and colonization.

To this Monroe added a blunt warning: any foreign attempt to colonize the western hemisphere in the future or to interfere in its business would be viewed as a hostile act toward the United States. *

Though the argument on behalf of the Monroe Doctrine put an end to the Nicaraguan-Dutch plan, it did nothing to deter a number of other countries, among them France and Great Britain. Both nations felt too powerful at the time to pay heed to the Doctrine. Starting in 1825, France spent almost two decades exploring possible canal locations in both Nicaragua and Panama. Nor was young Colombia troubled by the Doctrine. Its liberator and first president, Simon Bolívar, devoted many years to negotiating with France and Great Britain to have one or the other forge a canal across his country's Panamanian Isthmus.

Again, none of these dealings saw one spade of earth turned. But they did mark the start of a major change. They began to shift the focus of attention from Nicaragua to what would eventually become the site of the canal—Panama.

AMERICA STEPS FORWARD

The United States was also interested in the canal.

The fact is, there had been some American interest long before Alexander von Humboldt produced his canal

---

* The United States said that the Monroe Doctrine did not apply to already-established European colonies in the western hemisphere.

President James Monroe (standing) and his advisers appear in this romanticized painting commemorating the birth of the Monroe Doctrine.

writings. In the late 1700s, a future president—Thomas Jefferson—argued in favor of an American-built waterway. Humboldt's writings then triggered a wider interest. From about 1820 onward, not a year passed without the U.S. Congress debating the possibility of financing and building a canal across either Nicaragua or Panama. But problems such as the lack of money kept the Congress from advancing the idea beyond the talking stage. Regardless of those problems, however, United States interest so sharpened over the years that it finally resulted in a number of actions by both government and private financiers. Some of the most important of these actions took place during the years between 1846 and 1850.[5]

The Bidlack Treaty
Though the Colombian government had long been negotiating with the French and British for a canal across Panama, it was also interested in dealing with the United States. This interest resulted in a treaty in 1846. That year, American diplomat Benjamin A. Bidlack arranged a pact with Colombia that gave the United States the right to send, without charge, goods and persons along any roadway, railroad, or waterway that it might forge across the Isthmus. In return, the United States guaranteed the neutrality of the Isthmus. This meant that America would help protect the Isthmus against any foreign intrusion and would not itself interfere in Panamanian affairs. The United States also guaranteed that Colombia would retain its sovereignty over Panama.

America Spreads West
Long before the Bidlack Treaty was signed, many American pioneers had been making good use of the Isthmus. As the U.S. expanded westward during the first half of the 1800s, a growing number of settlers left the eastern states

and headed west to the Pacific coast. They found that they could travel any of three routes to their destinations: they could cross the continent by wagon train; they could board ships on the Atlantic coast and sail down around the foot of South America; or they could sail to Panama, cross the Isthmus, and pick up a ship for the final run up the Pacific.

Many travelers chose the third route because it promised to be the shortest and easiest of the lot. So many opted for that route, in fact, that a group of New York financiers decided a fine profit could be made from building a railroad across the Isthmus. The financiers formed the Panama Railroad Company in 1847 and gained permission from Colombia to build the line. The first tracks were laid in 1850 and the job was completed five years later.

In 1848, just after the formation of the railroad company, the California gold rush burst upon the scene and fired the imaginations of people everywhere. Hoping for quick riches, countless Americans along with adventurers from throughout the world swarmed to the gold fields. Thousands of Americans chose the Isthmus route. More than anything that had happened before, the gold rush convinced the United States of just how profitable a Panama waterway could be. Between 1848 and 1869, some 375,000 persons crossed Panama from the Caribbean to the Pacific. During those years, about 225,000—most of whom had either found nothing but hardship in California or had lost their gold dust in the gambling halls of some mining camp—made the crossing in the opposite direction as they trekked home in disappointment.

A New Pact
The year 1850 marked the signing of an important canal treaty between the United States and Great Britain.[6] It was called the Clayton-Bulwer Treaty, developed by the

American Secretary of State John Clayton and the British diplomat Sir Henry Bulwer. The history of the agreement can be traced to the 1700s when Spain's hold on the New World was weakening. Taking advantage of that situation, Britain had moved into the Caribbean and secured footholds along broad stretches of the Central American coast. (One foothold eventually became British Honduras, an area that remained a British holding until it became the independent nation of Belize in 1981.)

Among the shorelines claimed by Britain was that of Nicaragua. Since Nicaragua had long been a leading candidate as a site for the Atlantic-Pacific canal, the British announced plans to construct the waterway there. In the eyes of the Americans, the whole idea violated the Monroe Doctrine and so disturbed them that it brought the United States to the brink of war with England. The Clayton-Bulwer Treaty was intended to end the problem by making sure that the United States had some control in the building and welfare of a canal.

Under the terms of the treaty, the two nations agreed that, should a canal ever be built in Nicaragua or Panama, they would act together in its development and construction. Each promised the other not to construct the canal by itself, not to seek control over the waterway, and not to erect fortifications along its length. Both further agreed to keep the canal neutral in the event of war and leave it open to their ships.

★ ★ ★

Inch by inch, the United States seemed to be moving toward the day when it would build—or participate in building—the Atlantic-Pacific waterway. Then, suddenly, in the 1870s, there was a new development. France stepped in with a plan that promised to put the United States out of the canal picture for good.

[4]
AMERICA TAKES OVER

The early 1870s saw France more interested than ever before in building the Atlantic-Pacific waterway.[1] Its increased interest stemmed from the fact that it had just lost a war with Germany (the Franco-Prussian War, 1870–1871). France felt that its prestige had been severely damaged in the eyes of nations everywhere. There seemed only one certain way to restore its former glory. It would undertake and complete one of history's most challenging engineering projects—the linking of the world's two greatest oceans.

Toward this end, the French studied both Nicaragua and Panama for possible canal sites. Panama was finally chosen, in part because it was far narrower than Nicaragua and thus promised fewer problems for the builders. The French then successfully negotiated with Colombia for permission to lay the waterway across its possession.

The cost of building the canal was estimated at 1,174 million francs (at that time, the equivalent of $214 million). The French decided that government funds were not to be spent on the project so that they could be saved for other purposes. Instead, the work was to be financed by private investors on the promise that they would profit from the fees to be charged to ships for using the passage. A private company was formed in 1879 to raise the needed capital and then to undertake the construction itself. Appointed as president of the company was one of the most famous Frenchmen of the day, Ferdinand de Lesseps.

FERDINAND DE LESSEPS AND HIS CANAL

Born near Paris in 1805, de Lesseps was 74 years old at the time he was named the company's president. He had behind him a long and distinguished career as a diplomat—a career that had reached astonishing heights when the Suez Canal had been built under his leadership.[2]

The Suez waterway, which was completed in 1869, was the talk of the world. An engineering marvel that speared its way through the hot desert sands of Egypt, it was doing for European ships bound eastward to Asia what the Panama Canal would do for ships traveling between the Atlantic and Pacific. The Suez Canal enabled the vessels to avoid a long voyage down around the foot of Africa. The ships now cut across the Mediterranean Sea to the canal entrance before entering the Indian Ocean for the final run to their Asian destinations.

Because of his Suez experience, de Lesseps seemed the perfect choice for the Panama task. But in reality he proved to be anything but ideal. He was a stubborn, vain, opinionated man who, though not himself an engineer, believed he knew better than the engineers under his command. These failings, along with such factors as the diseases rampant in Panama, turned his canal work into a catastrophe.

A Disaster in the Making

The disaster began to take shape early on, when de Lesseps refused to heed the first advice given by his engineers.[3] He planned to have the channel run south from the city of Colón on the Atlantic side to Panama City on the Pacific. En route, it would follow the course of the Chagres River for a time and then pass through the mountain range that ran along the length of Panama's spine. His engineers had no quarrel with the route because it passed through the range at a spot where the mountains dropped to their lowest elevations. Here, they were really hills rather than mountains. But the engineers saw a problem.

They pointed out that de Lesseps planned to run the waterway through one of the highest of the hills. The hill, which became known as the Culebra hill, stood some 300 feet (91.4 m) tall. The engineers urged him to equip the canal with *locks.* These are giant chambers that, on being filled with water, would lift the ships over the hill.

It was a sound idea, but de Lesseps turned it down. Instead he planned to build a sea-level canal, one that would need no locks. It would run along a flat plane from one ocean to the other. His workers would conquer the 300-foot-high Culebra hill by simply cutting a gorge through it. The gorge would wind through the hill for 8 miles (12.8 km). It would be 72 feet (21.9 m) wide at the bottom and, of course, would measure 300 feet (91.4 m) deep from top to bottom. The engineers gasped at the amount of excavated earth needed to fashion the gorge. They said it would add up to millions of cubic yards (millions of cubic meters) and tried to argue with the old man to change his mind—but to no avail.

The Disaster Comes to Pass

The French began digging the canal in 1881. There was trouble right from the start. First, the Chagres River proved to be a danger; it could be a gentle stream at one moment and then, with a sudden rain, become a raging torrent that threatened to wash away not only the workers but also their equipment. Next, each rainfall turned the ground into a glue-like mud that made work almost impossible. Men, supply wagons, and machinery—all became trapped in the muck.

The rains and the mud were bad enough. But there was something worse—something deadly. The French quickly learned that Panama was one of the world's unhealthiest places. Yellow fever and malaria had long attacked the people of the Isthmus. Now these illnesses raised havoc among the workers, all of whom were new to the region and especially vulnerable to its health hazards. These two diseases killed more than 22,000 of the Indians, Jamaicans, Chinese, and whites who worked on the canal. Dead were more than twice the number of men employed at any one time in the digging.

Finally, as de Lesseps's engineers had expected, the attempt to gouge the 300-feet-deep (91.4 m) path through Culebra hill turned out to be a tragic error. The path was now known to the frightened laborers as the Culebra Cut. It was a terrifying place to work because the earth there proved unstable; it broke loose constantly, triggering landslides that sent tons of mud crashing down on the work crews. Seeming to dig only inches a day, teams of workers fought the hill for six years. By the end of that time, they had dug out 25 million cubic yards (18.7 million cubic meters) of earth, but still had another 240 feet (73 m) to go before reaching bottom. De Lesseps, now 82 years old, had to admit that he had made a terrible mistake. A sea-

Ferdinand de Lesseps

*Ferdinand's Folly: France's dream to build the first
Atlantic-Pacific waterway ended with the collapse
of de Lesseps's Panama Canal project, as lampooned
in this cartoon published in 1886.*

level canal would never work. He began to lay plans to install locks along the waterway.

Those plans, however, never materialized. By 1887, de Lesseps's company had run out of money and was unable to raise additional funds. Much of the original capital had come from everyday French citizens who had invested their modest savings in the project with the hope of not only earning a profit but also of bringing new glory to their country. Now, the French people—rich and poor—refused to waste another penny on the project. They all saw it as a doomed enterprise.

And doomed it was. The French abandoned the project in 1889 and departed from Panama. By then, despite all the problems encountered along the way, they had managed to finish two-fifths of the waterway. De Lesseps was left an old and defeated man, humiliated and widely criticized for failing to link the world's two greatest oceans. He died in 1894 at age 89.

With the French endeavor lying in ruins, it was now America's turn to step forward and take center stage in the canal drama.

AMERICA'S GROWING INTEREST

As you'll recall, the United States and Great Britain had in 1850 signed the Clayton-Bulwer Treaty, the agreement under which they promised to work together should one or the other decide to build an Atlantic-Pacific canal. In the years following the signing, interest in the waterway continued to blossom in the United States.[4] Congress annually discussed the possibility of allocating money for the project. But the job of building a connection between the two oceans was still too costly for such a young nation.

There was also much talk in Congress and at the

White House as to where the waterway should be placed. Suggested sites for its location ranged all the way from Mexico on the north to Panama on the south; of greatest interest were possible routes across Nicaragua or Panama.

In addition, there were numerous suggestions as to *how* the waterway should be built. Some engineers advised a lock canal to lift ships past any mountains or hills that might stand in the way. Others envisioned sea-level canals that would run as tunnels cut through the mountains. The oddest of all the suggestions came from an American engineer named James Eads. He drew plans for a railroad across Mexico's Isthmus of Tehuantepec. The railroad was to transport fully laden ships from coast to coast on cars equipped with giant platforms.

De Lesseps's effort to dig the waterway across Panama triggered two reactions in the United States. First, there was anger because the French canal posed a threat to the Monroe Doctrine. Second, de Lesseps's work did nothing to dampen the American desire to build a canal on its own one day, but it did cause the nation's leaders to focus their attention on an alternative Nicaraguan route.

In Washington, D.C., the anger felt for de Lesseps turned to glee when his work ended in failure. The interest in building a Nicaraguan canal intensified in Congress and at the White House. Still, no money was set aside for it. The job continued to loom as too expensive.

AMERICA TAKES OVER:
FIVE DEVELOPMENTS

During the years between 1898 and early 1904, five developments transformed America's interest in the canal from talk to action. These developments swung the nation's eyes from Nicaragua and settled them on Panama for good. And they led to Panama's emergence as an independent nation and to the United States construction of the canal across the Isthmus. The developments began with a war.

A War in Two Seas
In 1898, the United States plunged into the Spanish-American War. The conflict, triggered in part by American resentment over Spain's treatment of its Cuban possession, was fought in two widely separated areas—Cuba in the Caribbean and the Philippine Islands in the Pacific. Although the fighting lasted only a few months, it demonstrated that America needed a waterway that would enable her warships to move quickly from ocean to ocean to protect the holdings netted as a result of the conflict—the Philippines and Guam. At the height of the war, the battleship *Oregon* was called to Cuba. But the ship was docked in Seattle and it had to make a wild dash of 13,000 miles (20,920 km) around South America to reach the Caribbean. Every national leader clearly saw how a canal would have hastened the trip, and how it could hasten future military maneuvers.

Viewing the canal now as a necessity, the government in Washington formed a special commission in 1899 and ordered it to find a definite route—either in Nicaragua or elsewhere—for the waterway. At about the same time, Congress began discussing a bill that would allocate $180 million for the digging of a Nicaraguan canal. Talk was beginning to change to action.

The French Make an Offer
While the bill was being considered, the French replaced de Lesseps's company with a new firm. The new company, which was formed to recoup some of the losses suffered by de Lesseps, approached the United States with an unexpected proposal.

The company announced that it wanted to sell all of

its Panamanian holdings, including its equipment and the stretch of the canal that had already been dug. In 1901, it offered these holdings to the United States for just over $100 million.

Washington, still angry with the French for threatening the Monroe Doctrine, refused the offer—but made a counter offer. America would take over the holdings for a much smaller amount: $40 million. It would do so, however, only after it had received permission from Colombia to dig in Panama.

The company officials were appalled at the counter offer. It added up to far less than half of what they wanted. But the company had approached other nations in search of a sale and had not found one interest. And so, recognizing that "half a loaf was better than none," the French accepted the counter offer.

The United States government realized that it was being handed a splendid bargain. For a mere $40 million, at the very time it was thinking of spending $180 million on a Nicaraguan crossing, it was being given the chance to take over a canal that was two-fifths dug. But before paying the French, Washington undertook two steps— one with Great Britain and one with Colombia.

A New Treaty with England
First, the U.S. wanted to be rid of the Clayton-Bulwer Treaty. For years, the treaty had been detested by many American leaders. They felt that, in keeping with the Monroe Doctrine, the waterway should be built and maintained by the United States alone. Now, with the country moving steadily toward the day when digging might actually begin, they argued that Britain should not have equal rights in the canal's construction and maintenance. The U.S. government then began to talk with the British about cancelling the treaty.

To everyone's surprise, Great Britain liked the idea. Why? Because the country was caught up in the Boer War in South Africa. Under the terms of the Clayton-Bulwer agreement, it would have to share in providing money and manpower for the digging. Britain had neither to spare at the time.

In 1901, the treaty was replaced by a new agreement, the Hay-Pauncefote Treaty. Named for its developers— statesmen John Hay of the United States and Julian Pauncefote of England—it called for Great Britain to give the United States the right to act independently in the development of an Atlantic-Pacific waterway. Further, Britain agreed that the United States could close the canal to British shipping if it so desired in times of war. The United States, for its part, promised to keep the canal open to the shipping of all nations in times of peace and to charge an equal fee to all ships using the water passage.

The Colombian Problem

The United States next turned to Colombia to apply for permission to dig in Panama. In 1902, John Hay, who was then U.S. Secretary of State under President Theodore Roosevelt, opened negotiations with the Colombian government. The talks ended successfully in January 1903, with the signing of the Hay-Herran Treaty which granted to the United States a strip of land 6 miles (9.6 km) wide along the general route laid out by de Lesseps. Given to the U.S. was the right to administer and police this zone. In return, the U.S. was to pay Colombia $10 million. After the completed canal had been in operation for nine years, the U.S. would then pay Colombia an annual fee of $250,000.

Before the treaty could take effect, it had to be ratified by the Congresses of both Colombia and the United States. The U.S. Congress gave its approval in March

1903. But the Colombian Congress balked and said that not enough money was being paid for the right to dig in Panama. The Colombians demanded a payment of $15 million from the Americans and $10 million from the French. They also rejected many points concerning the future administration of the canal zone by the Americans.

The Colombian demands infuriated President Theodore Roosevelt—and the people of Panama.

Panama Revolts Again

Panama, you'll recall, had decided to remain a part of Colombia when it broke free of Spain in 1821.[5] But, in the following decades, the Isthmus holding turned out to be troublesome. Because many of the Panamanian people chafed under a distant ruler and wanted their land to be an independent nation, they had tried to break away from Colombia five times in the years between 1846 and the end of the nineteenth century, but had failed. Then, when the de Lesseps canal project had brought money to the Isthmus, the people had staged riots to keep the Colombian government's representatives from taking a lion's share of the newly arrived wealth.

In July 1903, on hearing that the Colombian Congress was opposing the canal treaty—thus threatening to choke off the wealth and jobs that the American digging promised—the Panamanian people again erupted in anger. In Panama City, a revolutionary committee of eight political leaders took shape and planned a new bid for freedom. Many historians believe it was a bid that the United States not only favored but helped to bring about. When the committee began mobilizing troops for an uprising, money to pay for their arms was quietly raised in both Washington and New York.

Sensing a rebellion in the making, the Colombian government sent 500 troops to Panama. They were to sail to the city of Colón on the Caribbean side of the Isthmus and then march overland to the seat of the uprising, Panama City. But now America's support of the revolt came fully to light. President Roosevelt ordered U.S. warships to Panama City and sent the gunboat *Nashville*, with a detachment of Marines aboard, to Colón.

The *Nashville* made port ahead of the Colombian troops. When the Colombians arrived, the ship's captain allowed their officers to cross the Isthmus, but prevented the troops from doing so. The captain said that he was making sure that the rights once given to the United States under the Bidlack Treaty for free passage across Panama were not endangered by any fighting.

And so, under the guise of protecting its rights of free passage, the United States kept the Colombian troops in Colón, and thus ensured the success of the rebellion. Without bloodshed, the Panamanian revolutionary forces took over the government offices in October and the opening days of November. On November 3, 1903, Panama declared itself an independent nation. Three days later, the United States formally recognized it as such.

At the same time the revolution was taking place, the United States paid the $40 million due the French and began to negotiate with a Panamanian representative, Philippe Bunau-Varilla, for permission to dig the canal. He and Secretary of State John Hay signed the Hay–Bunau-Varilla Treaty on November 18, 1903. Ratified by the U.S. Congress in 1904, the pact called for Panama as an independent nation to grant the Americans the right to build the canal across its territory.

★ ★ ★

Just six years had elapsed since the Spanish-American War convinced the United States that it must build an Atlantic-Pacific connection. Now, the French and Colom-

Secretary Shaw authorizes the release of $40 million for the Panama Canal. Although considered a "steal," the French company's final price tag for its Panamanian holdings was the largest sum ever paid by the U.S. Treasury at that time.

bians were gone from the Isthmus and out of the canal picture. Panama, after generations of dissatisfaction as a Colombian holding, was an independent nation. And the United States was ready to start work on what was to be called the Panama Canal, a waterway that would lock the histories of the two countries together for years to come.

[5]
A CANAL IS BUILT

In some ways, the Hay–Bunau-Varilla Treaty was identical to the Hay-Herran Treaty. [1] For example, the United States received permission to dig the Canal in exchange for a payment of $10 million to Panama. The U.S. also agreed to pay Panama a yearly fee of $250,000 after the waterway had been in operation for nine years. (The fee was increased in later years.)

In another way, however, the two treaties differed. Under the original pact, the U.S. was granted control over a 6 mile-wide (9.6 km) strip of land along the length of the waterway. The Panama treaty extended the width of the strip to 10 miles (16 km), stretching it to 5 miles (8 km) on either side of the Canal. The strip, called the Panama Canal Zone, was to be fully controlled by the United States.

The Americans began work on the Canal immediately—in May 1904, just three months after the ratification of the Hay–Bunau-Varilla Treaty. The construction was finished ten years later, in 1914. During that time, the

A cartoon of Uncle Sam creating the
Panama Canal with a handsaw

United States had spent almost $367 million on the project.

What was opened to ship traffic in 1914 was a waterway that stretched about 40 miles (64 km) across the Isthmus from shore to shore, and about 50 miles (80 km) from Atlantic deep water to Pacific deep water.[2] The Canal followed the same course as de Lesseps's failed waterway. But it was totally unlike the de Lesseps sea-level effort.

To help ships pass through the mountain range that runs along the spine of Panama, the U.S. project featured two man-made lakes and a series of locks and dams. The locks raise and lower ships to and from the lakes, which are located on either side of the mountain range. The lakes themselves were created by the dams. River water collects behind the dams after flowing in from the surrounding areas.

The lakes serve two purposes. They provide the water needed by the locks and establish a water level that is well above sea level and thus assist the Canal in making its way more easily through the mountain range.

Six sets of locks were constructed—three on the Atlantic side of the mountain range and three on its Pacific side. Each set consists of double locks. One lock serves Pacific-bound ships, while the other handles traffic heading to the Atlantic. Altogether, then, there are twelve locks along the Canal route. The two man-made lakes are giant Lake Gatun on the Atlantic side of the range and little Lake Miraflores on the Pacific side.

A JOURNEY
THROUGH THE CANAL

The simplest way to understand what was carved across the Isthmus is to imagine that you are a passenger aboard a ship as it ventures through the Canal. We'll pretend that

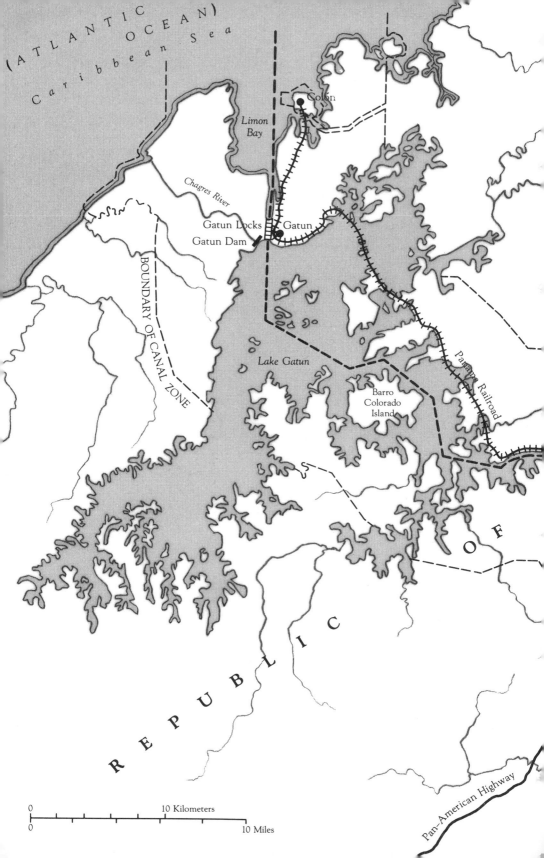

(ATLANTIC OCEAN)

Caribbean Sea

Limon Bay

Colón

Chagres River

Gatun Locks
Gatun Dam
Gatun

BOUNDARY OF CANAL ZONE

Lake Gatun

Barro
Colorado
Island

Panama Railroad

R E P U B L I C

O F

Pan-American Highway

0   10 Kilometers

0   10 Miles

PANAMA CANAL: CANAL ZONE AND VICINITY

you are traveling from the Atlantic to the Pacific. You'll spend between seven and eight hours on the waterway.

Your journey begins at Limon Bay alongside the city of Colón and carries you along a channel that was cut through the valley of the Chagres River. The channel, which is 500 feet (152 m) wide at its bottom, runs southward for 6²/₃ miles (10.7 km). (Because Panama stretches from east to west, always remember that the Panama Canal travels from northwest to southeast rather than, as is commonly believed, from east to west.) The channel ends at the Gatun locks.

The Gatun Locks

Dead ahead now are three locks that, coming one after the other, form a gargantuan staircase that rises to Lake Gatun. (Off to your side, of course, are their companions for ships moving in the opposite direction.) On traveling through the three locks, which are called sea chambers, your ship moves forward for more than half a mile (.8 km) and is lifted 85 feet (26 m) to the lake. Each lock is 1000 feet (304.8 m) long, some 70 feet (21.3 m) deep, and 110 feet (33.5 m) wide. Each can hold about 66 million gallons (250 million l) of water. All the locks along the Canal are, with some variation, the same size.

A ship always approaches the Canal locks with the help of a pilot and tugboats. Then, to safeguard against a costly accident, such as crashing into one of the side walls, cables are lashed to the ship as it enters the lock. The cables stretch upward to small locomotives—nicknamed *mules*—that chug along tracks atop both walls. They carefully pull the ship into place. Once your ship is in place and held securely by the cables, giant gates swing shut behind you.

The gates consist of two leaves—or doors. Each leaf is

65 feet (19.8 m) wide and 7 feet (2 m) thick. The leaves on the various Canal locks range in height from 47 feet 4 inches (14.5 m) to 82 (25 m) feet. Weighing from 370 to 730 tons (335 to 662 t), they are built of steel girders, contain inner compartments made of concrete, and are covered with steel sheathing. The doors hang on monstrous hinges. You'll see the largest of the gates after crossing Lake Miraflores. The gates on the lower locks there are the ones that hit the 730-ton (662 t) mark. They stand 82 feet (25 m) tall—the height of a six-story building.

After the gates have swung shut, water pours into the lock. It enters through culverts that pass through the lock walls and have their outlets in the lock floor. Slowly, your ship rises with the water and is lifted to the level of the next lock. Up ahead, giant gates open, allowing you to enter the second lock, and then swing shut again. Water now flows into the second lock for your ascent to the third lock. There is another trip upward and another opening of the lock doors up ahead. You enter Lake Gatun.

Lake Gatun

Lake Gatun covers an area of 164 square miles (425 sq. km). The lake was created by the construction of an earth-and-rock dam at the Gatun locks. The dam, which is built across the valley of the Chagres River, is 1½ miles (2.4 km) long at its top and a half-mile (.8 km) thick at its base. At base level, the dam wall is 400 feet (122 m) thick. From there, it narrows to 100 feet (30.5 m) thick at its top. Actually, it is two dams in one because there is a hill of rock at its center. The dam is built in two sections that are anchored to this rocky hill and stretch away from it in either direction.

Your ship follows a channel that has been cut across Lake Gatun. The channel varies in width from 500 to

A cruise ship prepares
to enter a series of locks
on the Panama Canal.

1000 feet (152.4–304.8 m), and varies in depth from 45 to 87 feet (13.7–26.5 m). The channel runs for 24 (38.6 km) miles.

Several islands dot Lake Gatun. They are the tops of hills that were not completely covered when water from the surrounding region flowed in and formed the lake after the Gatun dam was built. The Canal channel takes your ship close past the largest island, the 3,600-acre (1,457 ha) Barro Colorado. *

The channel across Lake Gatun ends its 24-mile (38.6 km) run at the spot called Gamboa. ** You now enter one of the most historic stretches of the Canal—the Gaillard Cut.

The Gaillard Cut

The Gaillard Cut was once famous as the Culebra gorge that ended de Lesseps's dreams of a sea-level waterway. It is now named in honor of the army engineer who was in charge of its construction for the United States, Col. David D. Gaillard.

The Cut twists through the hills for 8 miles (12.8 km). Its channel is 45 feet (13.7 m) deep and has a bottom width of 300 feet (91.4 m). Some ships today are so big

---

* When water first began to collect in the lake, the animals took refuge on the rapidly forming island. In time, the island was designated a natural reservation and, since the 1920s, has been used for biological research. Today, Barro Colorado boasts an animal population of at least 70 species of mammals, 1,200 types of spiders, 62 types of reptiles, and 3,000 forms of plant life.

** A river flows into Lake Gatun from the northeast at Gamboa. It comes from Lake Madden, which was formed in 1938 when Madden Dam was built. That dam measures about 974 feet (296.8 m) in length and 223 feet (68 m) in height. Madden Lake, which covers approximately 22 square miles (57 sq. k), serves as a reservoir. It supplies needed water when Lake Gatun's water level drops during dry periods.

that the Canal, especially here in the Cut, must be cleared of traffic moving in the opposite direction. The ships are too wide to get past oncoming vessels.

The Pacific Locks
and Lake Miraflores

Your passage through the Gaillard Cut at last brings you to the Pacific side of the mountain range and ends at the Pedro Miguel locks (one lock each for ships bound in opposite directions). The lock on your side lowers you 31 feet (9.4 m) to Lake Miraflores. Now at an elevation of 54 feet (16.4 m) above sea level, you cross the mile-wide (1.6 k) lake to the Miraflores locks.

At the Pedro Miguel locks, the water level in the Gaillard Cut is held in check by the locks themselves and two dams that extend away to hills on either side of the Canal. The combined length of the two dams is around 2,000 feet (610 m).

There are four locks at the far end of Lake Miraflores (again, two in either direction) and two dams that wall off the lake. The dams are located on either side of the locks; the one on the east side is built of concrete, while its companion on the west side is made of rock and earth. Together, they measure over 2,800 feet (853 m) in length. The west dam is the longer of the two. It runs for 2,300 feet (700 m).

The Miraflores locks lower you to sea level in two steps for the final leg of your journey to the Pacific. Less than 10 miles (16 km) away is the Pacific's deep water.

BUILDING THE CANAL:
THE PREPARATIONS

Though work on the Canal began in 1904, the actual digging did not begin for almost three years.[3] The time between 1904 and early 1907 was spent preparing for the job. The preparations were carried out along several fronts.

First, all the needed equipment—everything from hand shovels, crowbars, and pickaxes to giant steam shovels, dredges, and pile drivers—was shipped to the Isthmus. Arriving also were the thousands of vehicles and vessels that would be required to move equipment, men, and excavated earth from place to place. Among the arrivals were railroad locomotives, open freight cars, small rowboats, steamboats, and tugs. Panama's railroad tracks were repaired for use by the locomotives and cars.

Next, a variety of buildings took shape along the Canal route. Hammers rang out daily as offices, construction shacks, repair shops, hospitals, and living quarters for the workers rose from the muddy soil.

A government was established for the 10-mile-wide (16 km) Canal Zone. It was a government that would be needed not only during the construction period but in the subsequent years when hundreds of employees would work and live in the Zone while operating the Canal. Also established were police and fire departments, a court system, a customs and revenue service, and a postal system.

One of the most important pre-construction efforts centered on safeguarding the health of the thousands of men who would dig the Canal. This work was carried out by a U.S. Army Medical Corps officer, Col. William Crawford Gorgas.

Gorgas and
Disease Control

As you'll recall from Chapter 4, two tropical diseases—yellow fever and malaria—ran rampant among the de Lesseps work crews and killed more than 22,000 workers. The French were unable to check the two killers because they had no idea what caused them.

By the time Col. Gorgas went to work on the Canal,

Some fifteen years after the French abandoned the Canal project, chief engineer John F. Wallace tried to utilize de Lesseps's outdated equipment. Here, Jamaican laborers make use of old French handcars while excavating one of the Pedro Miguel locks.

the causes of both malaria and yellow fever had been determined.[4] In 1898, a British army surgeon, Dr. Donald Ross, discovered that malaria is transmitted to humans by the bite of the *Anopheles* mosquito. Two years later, an American army medical team proved that yellow fever is transmitted via the bite of the *Aedes* mosquito. The American medical team, which was directed by Col. Walter Reed, was working in Havana, Cuba, when it made its discovery. The team had been sent there to look into the disease because it afflicted so many of the United States troops stationed in Cuba during the Spanish-American War.

Gorgas, who was born in Mobile, Alabama, in 1854, was the United States Army's chief sanitation officer in Havana at the time of the yellow fever discovery. Armed with the identity of the villain responsible for the disease, he set out to eradicate yellow fever by wiping out the *Aedes* mosquito. He did this by attacking the insect's breeding ground—standing water. Working in and around Havana, he drained stagnant water from ponds, swamps, ditches, streams, gutters, and even the muddy pools that had gathered beneath houses. He ordered that all rain barrels and other water containers be covered with lids. His efforts were so successful that, in a matter of months, yellow fever virtually disappeared from Havana.

Because of his success in Cuba, the army sent Gorgas to Panama as soon as the pre-construction work began. He operated just as he had in Havana. Wherever possible, he drained lakes, swamps, ponds, streams, ditches, and puddles of their standing water. Water that could not be drained away was covered with oil to kill the mosquitoes, their eggs, and their larvae. Also, he ordered that all buildings be raised above the ground to keep their undersides clear of the damp surface and that the porches, doors, and windows of all buildings be fitted with screens.

*President Theodore Roosevelt on an
inspection tour of the Panama Canal*

Because of Gorgas's efforts, yellow fever was all but gone from the Panama Canal Zone by the time the digging began. Malaria also slowly faded over the years. By 1914, it posed little or no threat to the workers.

Many historians believe that the work of William Crawford Gorgas ranks high among the reasons why the Americans were able to build the waterway that had defeated de Lesseps. Gorgas remained on the job throughout the building of the Canal. In 1914, he was promoted to the rank of brigadier general and was named Surgeon General of the United States. He died in 1920 at age 66.

Two Decisions

While the preparations for the construction were under way, two decisions were being reached in Washington. First, President Theodore Roosevelt elected to have the Canal built by the government rather than private contractors. Second, despite all that had happened to the de Lesseps project, there was still much discussion about whether a sea-level or lock-equipped passage should be built. In 1907, the government opted for a lock-equipped project, thinking it to be a more practical choice in light of de Lesseps's experience. *

BUILDING THE CANAL: THE CONSTRUCTION

Once the two decisions were made, the government estimated that nine years would be needed to dig a lock canal

---

* The 1907 decision has since been questioned by United States leaders and engineers, with many thinking that America could have succeeded where de Lesseps failed and that a sea-level canal would have been a wiser choice in the long run. A sea-level canal could have better handled the extremely large ships that came into use over the years. As we'll see later, there have been several moves to replace the Canal with a sea-level waterway.

Col. George W. Goethals (center foreground) heads
the Isthmian Canal Commission. Left to right:
Major William Sibert, Senator Joseph Blackburn,
Rear Admiral Harry Rousseau, Joseph Bucklin Bishop,
Lt. Col. H. F. Hodges, Col. William C. Gorgas,
and Lt. Col. David Gaillard.

across the Isthmus.⁵ Actually, the job took just seven years to complete. It was done under the supervision of a government body called the Isthmian Canal Commission. In turn, two civilian engineers, John F. Wallace and John F. Stevens, headed the commission and served as the Canal's chief engineers during the preparations phase. In 1907, Col. George W. Goethals of the United States Army Corps of Engineers took over from them. He remained in charge throughout the construction phase, providing the leadership that saw one massive construction problem after another solved.

Under Goethals, the construction itself was accomplished by three simultaneous crews advancing toward each other so that the canal would be completed when they all finally met. Each crew consisted of thousands of men. The crews were named according to where they worked along the Canal route. There was the Atlantic crew, the Pacific crew, and the Central crew. What they did daily staggered the imagination of the watching world.

Their hand-shovels, pickaxes, dynamite, and giant steam shovels tore out millions of tons (millions of metric tons) of earth as they dug the channels along the Chagres River, across what was to become Lake Gatun, and through the Gaillard Cut. More than one hundred steam shovels worked along the route. The excavated earth was hauled away to dump sites by train. Some 110 locomotives and more than 2,000 open freight cars were used to cart the dirt away. Before the Canal was completed, more than 239 million cubic yards (183 million cubic m) of earth had been scooped up. Much of this soil was used for the earth-and-rock dams at Gatun and Miraflores.

To build the locks at Gatun, Pedro Miguel, and Miraflores, giant cement-mixing machinery was installed at the sites. Once mixed, the cement was carried in buckets along a network of overhead cables to the lock forms. Just

*Workmen pose in front of two concrete mixers
on the floor of one of the Miraflores locks.*

over 2 million cubic yards (1.5 million cubic m) of cement went pouring into the Gatun locks to fashion their walls and floors. Together, the Pedro Miguel and Miraflores locks swallowed another 2.4 million cubic yards (1.8 million cubic m).

Working Conditions

The working conditions along the emerging Canal were savage. The men labored under a blazing sun and in thick humidity. They constantly faced the danger of the floods and landslides that Panama's sudden and heavy rains could bring. They worked to the unending and deafening roar and clatter of machinery. Constantly, the air shook with the dynamite blasts that cleared dirt and rock from the Canal's path. At night, many of the men drank and gambled to forget their exhaustion and the hardships they endured daily. Some men cracked under the strain. Some went insane. Many quit and went home. Because of the turnover, the Canal ended up employing some 250,000 workers before it was finished.

At the height of construction, the Canal project had 50,000 men working on the job at the same time. They came principally from the United States, the islands of the Caribbean, and such European countries as England, France, Germany, Italy, Greece, Norway, and Sweden.

Though bad all along the route, the working conditions were at their worst in the Gaillard Cut. Two giant work crews, hacking their way toward each other from opposite sides of the Cut, labored not only in deafening noise but in a heat more intense and suffocating than that found at any other point along the Canal. The heat, which locked itself in the ever-deepening gorge, was generated by sunlight reflecting from the mountain walls on either side. Worse, steam shot up from the ground underfoot. The monstrous Cut was causing the hill to settle. Rocks and

A flood temporarily halts construction
of the Pedro Miguel locks.

*The treacherous Gaillard (Culebra) Cut was
the site of the deepest excavated portion of the Canal.*

layers of earth were pushing against each other and creating a friction beneath the surface. The friction built up a heat that finally released itself as steam rising through fissures in the earth.

Echoing along the Cut daily were explosions of dynamite that tore the earth loose so that it could be removed; some 60 million pounds (23 million kg) of explosives were detonated in the course of the digging. Then there was the clatter of the drills that further loosened the earth. Next, there was the roar of some fifty monster steam shovels, each weighing 97 tons (88 t), that scooped up the earth in 5-ton (4.5 t) mouthfuls and dropped it onto railroad cars for the journey to the dump site. And, finally, there was the chug, clank, and bang of the trains as they carted their loads away. At one time during the digging, the trains made about 160 round trips a day between the Cut and the dump site.

On top of the noise and heat, there was the constant fear of landslides. Just as they had done in de Lesseps's day, the hills gave way and dumped tons of dirt down into the gorge, often ruining the digging of days and even weeks. In all, there were about thirty major landslides in the Cut before it was completed. The costs of the damaged equipment and extra digging they necessitated added up to $10 million.

A Waterway Takes Shape

Despite all the problems endured in the Cut and elsewhere, the Canal slowly and steadily took shape. The last year of construction, 1913, was a banner year. The dams and locks at either end of the route were completed in May. That same month, the two work crews that had spent years advancing toward each other finally met in the Gaillard Cut. Water was let into the Gatun locks from the mammoth man-made lake forming behind them. A

*Giant steam shovels and dredges were
used to scoop up tons of rock and earth.*

*Huge upper locks at Lake Gatun dwarf
laborers working on one of the lock's gates.*

On October 10, 1913, President Woodrow Wilson
sent the electric spark that blew up Gamboa Dike—
the Canal's last obstruction to sea-vessel navigation.

month later, the lake water was allowed to enter the Gaillard Cut; it had hitherto been kept out by means of dikes across the Cut. The next weeks saw water admitted into the locks at Pedro Miguel and Miraflores. A small work boat, the *Alexander La Valley*, made the first passage from one end of the waterway to the other on January 7, 1914.

The Panama Canal, dreamed of for centuries, was at last a reality. The Canal opened to sea traffic on August 15, 1914, and it ranked high among the world's most astonishing engineering feats. For it, the Isthmian Canal Commission adopted the motto: *A Land Divided, A World United*. Indeed, the world was now united by an easily reached link between its two greatest oceans.

★ ★ ★

But Panama and the United States were not to be united by the Canal. Because of it—and the zone through which it passed—the coming years were to be stormy ones for the two countries.

[6]
AN ANGRY PANAMA

From its opening day in 1914, the Panama Canal was enthusiastically welcomed by the world's sea trading nations. But it received a mixed greeting from the Panamanian people. Some liked having it in their midst. Others were angered by its presence.

THE CANAL AND
WORLD SHIPPING

The welcome given by the world's sea trading nations is best seen in the amount of cargo that was sent through the Canal.[1] In its first year of operation, vessels carrying 5 million tons (4.5 million t)* of cargo passed along the

---

* More than 5 million tons (4.5 million t) of cargo would have been shipped through the Canal during 1914 had there not been a major landslide in the Gaillard Cut that year. The Canal was closed until 1915 while the Cut was cleared of dirt and rock. Slides have continued to plague the Cut through the decades.

waterway. Eventually, the annual cargoes increased to 30 million tons (27 million t) by the 1950s.

In the 1960s, the annual cargoes jumped to over 60 million tons (54 million t) and, since then, have ranged up to a high of above 168 million tons (185 million t). In the 1980s, the annual cargoes have run upwards of around 145 million tons (152 million t). In the course of its history to date, more than a billion tons (billion t) of cargo have passed along in the Canal.

Depending on the world's political and economic conditions, the number of ships that travel through the Canal varies from year to year. For example, there was a dip in tonnage during World War II when the fighting interrupted international trade; conversely, the number of vessels rose significantly when the Suez Canal was closed in 1967 because of the Arab-Israeli War. At present 1,000 ships sail across the Isthmus each month—or roughly thirty ships a day.

In all, about 5 percent of the world's water shipping passes through the Canal. Its greatest user is the United States. Much of America's trade with its South and Central American neighbors travels via the waterway. Close behind the United States in use of the Canal is Japan.

A wide, almost endless, variety of goods has passed along the Canal. The principal commodities moving from the Pacific to the Atlantic include lumber, oil, bananas, steel, and iron. Ranking high among the goods traveling in the opposite direction are coal, oil, grains, and phosphates.

Ships pay tolls for the use of the Canal. The tolls have always been kept low to encourage use of the waterway. They vary and are based on several factors, among them the weight and type of vessel. Fees differ for fully laden merchant ships, empty freighters, passenger liners,

Flanked on both sides by lush countryside,
a ship sails through the Panama Canal.

and warships, with tolls averaging to more than $10,000 a transit.

THE CANAL AND THE PANAMANIAN PEOPLE

As mentioned, the Panamanians greeted the new canal with mixed feelings. Many welcomed it. Others were angered by it. Many vacillated between the two feelings.

Those who welcomed the waterway did so because it brought their country a variety of economic benefits.[2] For one, soon after the Hay–Bunau-Varilla Treaty was signed in 1903, an American payment of $10 million went to Panama. Then the U.S. began paying an annual fee— called an annuity—of $250,000 once the Canal had been in operation nine years. That annuity was later increased. Now it ranges up to $80 million annually.

The Canal prompted a number of American companies to invest in Panama. They bought land from the nation's rich landowning families for the purpose of going into business there. Unfortunately, this wealth did not filter down to the ordinary citizen but was kept in the hands of wealthy landowners.

However, there were also specific advantages for the ordinary citizen. As you know, the Hay–Bunau-Varilla Treaty gave the United States full control over the Canal and the Canal Zone. And so, until recently, both were run by two U.S.-sponsored organizations—the Zone government (to supervise such bodies as the police, postal, and court systems that were established during the pre-construction days) and the Panama Canal Company, which held responsibility for operating and maintaining the waterway. These two organizations were the major employers on the Isthmus. Between them, they have consistently employed between 10,000 and 13,000 civilian workers. When the work force stood at just over 13,000 in 1977, 3,500 employees were Americans and 9,600 were non-U.S. citizens. The non-U.S. workers were mainly Panamanians.

Many other Panamanians also profited from the waterway. Though not directly employed by the Canal, they sold goods and services to the Zone and its workers, the passing ships, and the 10,000 U.S. military troops (and their families) stationed in the Zone to protect the Canal. It has been estimated that the Canal has accounted for about 20 percent of Panama's employment.

As we'll see later, the running of the Canal is no longer solely in U.S. hands, but is now shared with Panama. The waterway nevertheless remains a major source of Isthmian employment. Because of an agreement made in 1977, the Canal will pass completely from the Americans to the Panamanians at the close of this century. It is expected to become an even greater employer of Panamanians as that time approaches.

But, despite all its economic benefits, many Panamanians were angered by the presence of the Canal in their midst.

AN ANGRY PANAMA

The anger dates back to the very first days of Panama's independence and the signing of the Hay–Bunau-Varilla Treaty.[3] The angry Panamanians called the pact grossly unfair. They felt that it was all in favor of the United States and would do their country nothing but harm.

The principal target of their fury was Philippe Bunau-Varilla, the man who had negotiated the treaty on Panama's behalf. Bunau-Varilla had been given the task of arranging the pact by the revolutionary committee that launched Panama's successful bid for freedom. But many

Panamanians charged that he had not worked on the committee's behalf at all, but against the group.

The Panamanian citizens began by pointing out that Bunau-Varilla was not even a citizen of Panama. Rather, he was a French businessman who had come to the Isthmus at the time de Lesseps was attempting to dig the Canal. He had stayed on after the French departed in failure. In 1903, when he worked out the treaty with U.S. Secretary of State John Hay, Bunau-Varilla had been much more than a representative of the revolutionary committee. He had also been in the employ of the French company that was to receive $40 million from the United States in exchange for the de Lesseps holdings.

Since the United States would not pay until it was sure that Panama would agree to having the Canal built, it was in the company's interest to have a treaty quickly arranged. Consequently, the Panamanians felt that Bunau-Varilla had not been interested in a fair deal for their country. They claimed that he had been interested only in a treaty so favorable to the United States that Secretary Hay would not argue about it and delay its passage. And Hay did as expected. He wasted no time in signing the pact. The U.S. Congress just as quickly approved it.

Bunau-Varilla was not the only target of Panamanian anger. The people sharply criticized the government of their new country for accepting the one-sided treaty. They charged that the government failed to use good judgment because it was blinded by two factors—first, the gratitude felt for the American help in the revolution and, second, the desire for the wealth that the Canal and its construction promised to bring to the Isthmus.

And there was anger directed at the United States. The Panamanians were as grateful as their government for America's help in winning their independence. But they could not forgive their giant neighbor for so quickly grabbing at an arrangement that they believed the American government had to know was both unfair and greedy. An anti-American rage started then that was to endure for years. It was true, the Panamanians admitted, that the Canal would benefit their economy. But their country was being made to give up far too much in exchange.

Exactly what, in their opinion, was Panama surrendering? For the answer, just listen to the complaints that were voiced during the Canal's construction and in the years following. Most of Panama's complaints were directed against the treaty agreements pertaining to the Canal Zone.

The Zone:
Size and Location
The very size and location of the Zone triggered an angry outcry. Ten miles (16 km) wide and some 50 miles (80.4 km) long, it embraced an area of 553 square miles (1,432 sq km)—an area that, totaling 5 percent of the nation's land mass, speared its way directly through the heart of Panama. The Panamanians complained that it chopped their already small country into two smaller pieces. The split would make it difficult, if not impossible, for Panama to grow as a single, united nation; and, with the Canal lying in their path, the people would have trouble moving from one side of the country to the other. Families and friends would be separated. Business would be difficult to conduct across the waterway. Political views might grow to be different on each side. In the end, Panama could well end up being *two* countries.

The Zone:
American Sovereignty
Even more galling to the Panamanians was the fact that the Hay–Bunau-Varilla Treaty not only gave the United States the right to occupy and use the Zone but also

granted the United States full sovereignty over it. *Sovereignty* means "the supreme power to rule; the power to rule without interference by any outside force."

The Panamanians saw clearly what this meant. The Americans could run the Zone as they saw fit, without advice from anyone. The government of Panama would have no say whatsoever in what went on there. After finally winning its independence, Panama was to have what amounted to a foreign country sitting in its very midst.

From the moment the treaty was signed, a number of Panamanian leaders demanded that the Zone be ruled by the country within which it lay. They said that the treaty's award of sovereignty to the United States must be interpreted a certain way. It must be viewed as meaning that the Americans were entitled to sovereign authority only in matters pertaining to the construction, maintenance, and protection of the Canal. The Panamanian leaders argued that in all other matters, Panama was to hold sovereignty.

Leaders in the United States disagreed. They interpreted the pact as granting the United States full sovereignty. Panama's sovereignty in the Zone, they said, was to be titular—meaning "in name only." The two countries were locked for years in an argument over which interpretation was correct. All the while, the United States ran the Zone on its own.

The matter of United States sovereignty was further troubling because it was granted in perpetuity, meaning forever. The shocked Panamanians said that their country was being made to endure the presence of an outsider for all time to come.

The Zone:
The Fear of Intervention
The Hay–Bunau-Varilla Treaty did more than just grant the United States the Canal Zone and full sovereignty over it. It also contained the following terms:

The United States guaranteed to preserve the independence of Panama.

So that it could protect the Canal, the United States had the right to step in and maintain order should there ever be trouble in the cities at either end of the waterway—Colón and Panama City.

The United States was entitled to take lands outside the Zone if they were needed for the defense of the Canal in times of war or Panamanian upheaval.

The guarantee to safeguard Panama's independence were it ever threatened by another nation was comforting, but the other two terms were infuriating. To the citizens of Panama, the terms meant that the United States had the right to intervene in Panama's affairs whenever it wished, even if there was no real need or reason for the interference. One term gave the Americans the freedom to take over the country's two major cities without invitation from the Panamanian government. The other term allowed them to grab land outside the Canal Zone without any permission whatsoever. In all, the Panamanians felt that the United States, in the name of protecting its Canal, had been given the excuse to do as it wished whenever it didn't like anything that was going on in their country.

The United States defended the terms by saying that it was supplying the money, equipment, and engineering skill necessary to build and run the Canal. The terms were prudent safeguards, meant to protect an enormous investment against the dangers posed by war, attacks on Panama from the outside, and political turmoil within the country.

It was an argument that fell on deaf ears. As far as many of the Panamanians were concerned, the entire pact added up to a monstrous insult. The treaty had turned their new nation into nothing more than an American possession.

The Zone:
Discrimination

Despite not liking the Hay–Bunau-Varilla Treaty, the Panamanians, certain that the Canal would bring them jobs, eagerly looked forward to the day when its construction would begin. But they were angered when the Americans began hiring the work force for the digging. They found that they were not wanted. Instead, the jobs went mostly to United States citizens, Europeans, and black laborers shipped in from the Caribbean islands, chiefly Jamaica. Only a few Panamanians managed to land jobs.

When confronted by the Panamanian anger, the Americans had two answers. First, they said that most Isthmian people were of small physical stature and therefore not up to the heavy work the digging would require. Second, the Americans were worried about dealing with workers who spoke only Spanish. There could be delays, problems, and accidents because of the language barrier. On the other hand, the black laborers from Jamaica were welcome because they were sturdy and spoke English. And some of them had experience in the work that lay ahead because they had labored years earlier on the de Lesseps canal.

★ ★ ★

And so, regardless of its various economic benefits, the Canal was the source of what the Panamanians claimed to be many wrongs. Those alleged wrongs created a resentment that for years marked Panama with strife. But the strife led to a number of steps that attempted to right the wrongs and that ended with an agreement to remove the Canal from American hands.

[7]

RIGHTING THE WRONGS

Before we can talk of righting any U.S. wrongs in Panama, we must ask two questions. Were there actually wrongs to be righted? Were the Panamanians justified in their complaints?

The answer to both questions is "yes." To see why, let's look at some of the actions that resulted from the rights granted the United States in the Hay–Bunau-Varilla pact.

Intervention

There was good reason to fear intervention. The United States did intervene in Panama's affairs a number of times through the years.[1] For example, soon after the country declared its independence, the Indians in one area of Panama rebelled against some of the new government's policies. The United States sent troops into the area to keep the peace. They stayed for two years.

Another example: in 1925, the people of Panama City rioted against the high rents they were being charged for housing. The United States stepped in with six hundred troops. Advancing with fixed bayonets, the troops broke up a mob that was threatening to take over the city and thus earned the hatred of countless Panamanians. When General John J. Pershing, the commander of U.S. forces in World War I, visited Panama City that year, angry crowds hurled rocks at his car.

One thing, however, must be said in defense of the United States. It usually intervened only when asked to do so by the Panamanian government or by some political group that needed help.

Discrimination

The American reluctance to hire Panamanians to dig the Canal may have been truly based on their small physical stature and may have had nothing to do with racial or ethnic discrimination.[2] But, along with so many nations that held foreign possessions at the time, the United States did make the mistake of looking down on the people native to its holding. A number of discriminatory practices were long seen in the Canal Zone.

During the construction period, white workers were paid in gold while others received the less valuable metal, silver. Then, when the Panamanians were employed to help run the Canal once it was built, they were paid lower wages than their American fellow workers. The Panamanians were not allowed the same health and life insurance benefits that the Americans enjoyed and there were even separate drinking fountains for the American and Panamanian workers.

An American Possession

The Panamanians were correct in thinking that the Hay–Bunau-Varilla Treaty had virtually turned the Canal Zone into an American possession. There can be no doubt that the United States looked on the Zone as a possession and not a stretch of land that it shared with Panama. For many years, American schoolbooks listed it as a possession. U.S. leaders called it a possession. The American flag flew alone over the Zone until the 1960s. Only then was the Panamanian flag allowed to fly with it in acknowledgment of Panama's titular sovereignty there.

And there can be no doubt that the powers of intervention given to the United States by the treaty, plus the special U.S. provision in Panama's first constitution that we'll soon discuss, turned the whole nation into an American holding. That the entire country was dominated by the U.S. can be seen in three ways. During the first years of independence, U.S. officials supervised Panamanian elections. The Panamanian government routinely asked the United States for advice in various matters. And American officials were allowed to serve as advisers to Panamanian leaders.

RIGHTING THE WRONGS:
THE FIRST STEPS

In January 1904, political representatives from various parts of Panama met and drew up a constitution for the new nation.[3] It was to be the first of four constitutions under which the country has governed itself. New Panamanian constitutions were adopted in 1941, 1946, and 1972.

That first constitution was drawn along democratic lines and was modeled in great part after the U.S. Constitution. It called for a separation of powers among the branches of government and for a president to be elected by the people. Once the constitution was adopted, the committee that had led the revolution and governed the country since independence stepped aside. One of its members, Manuel Amador, was elected Panama's first president.

The new constitution pleased the Panamanian people, except for the provisions concerning the United States that it contained. Called Article 136, the provision granted the United States the right to intervene in any part of Panama to "reestablish peace and constitutional order." The Article further angered all those Panamanians already upset by the Hay–Bunau-Varilla Treaty. It strengthened the powers given in the treaty and did, indeed, turn their country into an American possession.

Article 136 so rankled the Panamanians that many wanted to rise in a new rebellion and cast the Americans out, Canal or no Canal. All heads of government in Panama from Amador onward objected to Article 136 and the Hay–Bunau-Varilla Treaty. They did not, however, listen to the demands to oust the Americans, but opted for a more prudent approach. Rather than risk an armed confrontation with the Americans, they sought over the years to have the Article and the treaty revised or dropped altogether through negotiations with the United States.

American Support
As those years came and went, a growing number of American leaders began to echo the Panamanian anger.[4] They knew that the Spanish-American War at the turn of the century had changed the United States greatly. The conflict, ending in victory for the United States, had gained the country its first overseas possessions—Guam, Puerto Rico, and the Philippine Islands—and had elevated it from a young and growing nation to a world power. They felt that their government, bloated with a sense of that new power, had selfishly taken unfair advantage of Panama in the Hay–Bunau-Varilla Treaty.

They now wanted to see the end of that injustice. And they wanted to put a stop to the nation's intervention in Panamanian affairs. It was earning their country nothing but dislike in Panama.

The growing clamor for fairness and non-intervention reached great heights in the 1920s. By then, the United States had gone on not only to intervene in Panama but also in the political upheavals of a number of other Latin American nations, among them the Dominican Republic and Nicaragua. The United States had done so, in part, to keep the peace and in part, to protect American business interests in these countries. But the interventions had made the United States a hated nation throughout Latin America. They had also prompted many Latins to say that the United States was trying to turn the Caribbean into an "American Lake."

No More Intervention

In 1928, President Herbert Hoover set about putting an end to the problem. He announced that the United States would now follow a policy of non-intervention in Latin American affairs. The policy, of course, was to apply to Panama as well as all the other Latin American states.

That Mr. Hoover meant what he said was seen just three years later. In Panama, a political action group called Accion Communal (communal action) charged the government of President Florencio Arosema with corruption and triggered a rebellion that ousted him from office in 1931. One of Accion Communal's leaders, Harmodio Arias, was elected president in his place. The U.S. government looked on Arosema's overthrow as an illegal seizure of a government and disliked Arias because he was strongly anti-American. But the United States did not once intervene in the upheaval.

When Franklin D. Roosevelt won election to the U.S. presidency in 1932, he continued Mr. Hoover's non-intervention policy and gave it a name—the Good Neighbor Policy. In line with the policy, he sent U.S. representatives to a conference of nineteen Latin American countries in 1933. At the close of the conference,

PANAMA CANAL

Bernard Partridge

Uncle Sam extends a cold elbow in this 1912 British
cartoon depicting U.S. intervention in Panama's affairs.

which was held in Uruguay, the nineteen nations all agreed not to interfere in each other's disputes and internal affairs. The United States joined them in the agreement.

Mr. Roosevelt's support of the Good Neighbor Policy stemmed from two roots. First, there was the President's own personal sense of right and justice. Second, at the time Mr. Roosevelt entered the White House, Adolf Hitler was rising to power in Germany. The President felt that the German dictator was sure to lead the world into war. He wanted to make certain that all the North, Central, and South American nations would stand united should his vision of the coming conflict come true—as it did when fighting broke out in Europe in 1939 and then in the Pacific in 1941.

A New Treaty

The Good Neighbor Policy opened the way to a new treaty between Washington, D.C., and Panama.[5] Called the Hull–Alfaro Treaty (for its negotiators, Secretary of State Cordell Hull and Panamanian representative Ricardo Alfaro), the pact was signed in 1936. In it, the United States gave up several of the rights granted by the Hay–Bunau-Varilla Treaty. The U.S. agreed to:

> *End its guarantee to protect Panama's independence.*
>
> *Surrender its right of unilateral intervention anywhere in Panama. This meant that America could no longer intervene on its own, but could do so only when asked by the Panamanian government.*
>
> *Give up its right to take lands outside the Zone in the event they were thought needed for the defense of the waterway. From now on, the U.S. would have to get permission before taking them.*

Finally, the United States raised the annual fee paid to Panama from $250,000 to $430,000.

The Panamanian people gave the Hull–Alfaro Treaty a mixed greeting. On the one hand, they were happy to see that these changes ended Panama's status as a United States possession. The people could now think of their country as an independent nation. But, on the other hand, the treaty left the Canal Zone under full U.S. sovereignty. Panama still had a foreign holding running right through its center.

RIGHTING THE WRONGS: THE SECOND STEP

In 1938, Harmodio Arias was replaced as Panama's president by his brother Arnulfo. Arnulfo proved to be as anti-American as Harmodio. His anti-Americanism was clearly seen in the opening days of World War II in Europe.[6]

At the time, the United States was still neutral in the conflict. Realizing that it might soon be drawn into war, the U.S. government wanted to establish additional military bases in Panama in case they were ever needed. Since the Hull–Alfaro pact made it impossible to seize land wherever it wished, Washington had to ask Panama's permission to set up the bases. Arias vehemently opposed the request.

The Panamanians feared the Hitler menace and saw their president's refusal of the U.S. request as dangerous— so dangerous that the country's military force, the National Guard,* overthrew Arias in 1941. Panama's National

---

* Panama did not have an army at the time. The National Guard served as the nation's military and police force. Today, Panama's military and police forces are known as the Panama Defense Force.

Assembly—its Congress—then appointed Roberto de la Guardia to the presidency. Under de la Guardia, Panama sided with the United States when the United States finally entered the world conflict in December 1941. During World War II, the Canal provided a speedy Atlantic-Pacific service for warships, troop ships, and freighters carrying military hardware and goods. Because of this service, the Canal enabled the United States to fight a war in two oceans with an efficiency that would have been otherwise impossible.

As we read on from here, one point must always be kept in mind. The National Guard has played a major role in Panama's political life ever since ousting Arias. It has overthrown a number of the nation's presidents and has then taken any of three actions. It has replaced the presidents with its own leaders as dictators; it has had men of its choosing named to the position by the National Assembly; or it has run candidates of its own in the presidential elections. As a result, Panama's leadership for years has bounced around among dictators, elected presidents, and appointed presidents.

Oddly enough, the first man overthrown by the Guard after World War II was again Arias. He staged a political comeback in the 1948 presidential race. The vote was so close that he claimed victory. But the Guard's leaders disputed his claim and placed their own presidential candidate in office. Arias made it to the presidency in 1949, but was once again deposed by the Guard. Then, in 1952, the Guard's candidate, Colonel José Arturo Remon, won the presidency.

The Eisenhower-Remon Treaty
Like the leaders before him, President Remon was solidly opposed to U.S. sovereignty over the Canal Zone. And so he pushed hard to have the Hay–Bunau-Varilla pact can-

celled. Starting in 1953, his representatives negotiated for two years with the administration of President Dwight D. Eisenhower. The result was the Eisenhower–Remon Treaty of 1955.[7] It was a pact that failed to end America's sovereignty in the Zone, but it did concede four points long sought by Panama. In the treaty, the U.S. agreed to:

Provide equal pay and working conditions for the Americans and Panamanians working in the Zone. This provision was aimed at ending the discriminatory practices that had long been seen in the Zone.

Increase the yearly Canal fee due Panama to $1,930,000.

Restrict the use of the Zone's stores and shops to the people—American and Panamanian alike—living inside the Zone. Ever since the first days of the Zone, anyone in Panama could purchase food and other merchandise from these stores. Since the stores charged low prices, they had been a financial help to the Panamanians. But the U.S. now agreed to curb their use after hearing numerous complaints that their low pricing was unfair to merchants outside the Zone.

Build a bridge across the Canal at the Pacific coast town of Balboa. The bridge helped to end the long-standing complaint that the Canal was dividing Panama in half and making it difficult for people to travel from one side of the waterway to the other to do business with anyone on its far side. The bridge, which cost $20 million, connected the east and west arms of the Pan-American Highway. Its construction was completed in the early 1960s.

★ ★ ★ ★

Years of negotiations between Panama and the United States had produced two treaties that corrected many of the wrongs the Panamanians felt were contained in the Hay–Bunau-Varilla pact. Panama had pushed hard to win the points granted to it in the two treaties. The United States had shown an understanding that it had intervened in the country's affairs, that it had been guilty of discriminatory practices in the Zone, and that it had acted unwisely in both cases.

But, no matter how many issues were settled by the two treaties, the Panamanians felt that two of their greatest problems with the United States remained. One concerned their flag; the other their desire to win full sovereignty over the Canal Zone.

Steps toward solving these problems began in 1959 with an outbreak of violence.

[8]

THE FINAL STEPS

The 1936 and 1955 treaties revealed Panama's strategy to rid itself of the hated Hay–Bunau-Varilla pact. In both instances, the little country bargained for the best terms it could get. Then, on securing all that could be won at the time, it agreed to the pacts. Each treaty gained a number of victories for Panama, after which the nation began new negotiations and went in search of further victories.

Once the Eisenhower–Remon Treaty was signed, only two major victories remained to be won. First, the United States had to be made to acknowledge Panama's titular authority in the Canal Zone by flying the Panamanian flag side by side with the American colors. Second— and this was the greatest goal of all—Panama had to be given full sovereignty over that massive stretch of land.

THE FLAG VICTORY

On May 2, 1958, a group of Panamanian students marched into the Canal Zone.[1] Angry over the continuing

failure to recognize their country's titular sovereignty, they carried seventy-two Panamanian flags and placed them at various spots. The Zone police quickly ejected the students. Public Panamanian reaction was just as quick. Anti-American rioting erupted outside the Zone.

More rioting followed the next year and resulted in forty people being injured. President Eisenhower then quieted things for a time by ordering that the Panamanian and U.S. colors be flown together in Shaler Triangle, a large plaza at the Panama City end of the Zone. Next, in 1962, President John F. Kennedy further relieved the problem when he agreed to fly the Panamanian flag at sixteen sites within the Zone.

But the matter brought one more upheaval. In early January 1964, students at an American high school in the Zone raised the American flag alone on their campus. Two days later, angry Panamanian students flooded onto the campus and attempted to run up their flag. The Americans and Panamanians began pushing each other. Within minutes, the melee turned into a full-scale riot that saw American cars and buildings burned.

The whole incident got so out of hand in the next three days that $2 million worth of damage was done to Zone property. Twenty Panamanians and four Americans were killed before quiet was restored. As a result of the tragic outburst, Panama broke off diplomatic relations with the United States on January 1965. Relations were not restored until the following April.

Student demonstrators burn the U.S. flag as a symbol of protest against American sovereignty over the Panama Canal Zone.

MORE NEGOTIATIONS

President Remon never lived to see his pact with President Eisenhower signed. He was assassinated by political enemies in 1955. Remon's supporters helped Ernesto de la Guardia succeed as president in 1956. La Guardia was followed into office by Roberto Chiari in 1961, with Marco Aurelio Robles then winning the presidential election of 1964, and the often-deposed Arnulfo Arias in 1968.

Arias remained in office just eleven days before again being overthrown by the National Guard, which had long opposed him politically. The Guard's leader, General Omar Torrijos, took the reins of government and he eventually assumed the powers of a dictator. Because of a series of reforms that he enacted to weaken the political power of the rich landowners and to help the poor, Torrijos won great support among the Panamanian people. In 1972, Panama's legislators declared him the country's "maximum chief" and adopted the nation's fourth constitution. In it, the legislators recognized his National Guard to be Panama's chief governing body.

From President Roberto Chiari onward, most of the Panamanian leaders negotiated with the United States on Canal matters, with the ultimate aim to win full sovereignty over the Zone.[2] For example, Mr. Chiari and President Kennedy worked together in the early 1960s. Their work bore fruit when President Kennedy signed an agreement calling for the Panamanian flag to be flown alongside the American flag at sixteen locations in the Zone. The agreement also called for Panama and the United States to continue working together to improve the pay of Panamanian employees in the Zone.

Next, from the mid- to late-1960s, the governments of Mr. Chiari and his successor, Marco Aurelio Robles, worked with President Lyndon B. Johnson on a treaty that Mr. Johnson wanted to see enacted. Tired of the anger that had marred Panamanian–U.S. relations since the dawn of the century, Mr. Johnson planned to cast aside the Hay–Bunau-Varilla pact and replace it with an agreement that would have both Panama and the U.S. share in the operation and defense of the Canal.

In addition, Mr. Johnson wanted the treaty to open the way to talks about replacing the Canal itself with a sea-level waterway. For years, the United States had been thinking about a sea-level connection for the Atlantic and Pacific. We'll see why later in this chapter.

Mr. Johnson saw the proposed pact as a daring and fair one because, unlike all the treaties of the past, it ended America's complete sovereignty over the Canal Zone. Panama was now to share in that sovereignty. Surely, the chief complaint that had been leveled at the United States for more than sixty years would now be eased, if not ended altogether.

But matters did not turn out as Mr. Johnson had hoped. The negotiations collapsed when the terms of the planned agreement (actually, the terms were contained in three separate treaties) were made public. They angered many people in both Panama and the United States. The idea of sharing in the operation and defense of the Canal failed to satisfy the Panamanians; they were still being denied complete sovereignty over the Zone. In the United States—in the streets and in Congress—there were strong objections to giving up even a portion of the American rights in the Zone. It was U.S. territory and should not be taken away. The Canal was an American-built-and-financed project. It should be run by Americans.

The collapse of the negotiations ended all Canal talks for the next three years. When they resumed in 1971, Panama had a new leader—General Omar Torrijos. His government would negotiate successfully for the treaty that completely changed the American role in Panama.

THE EIGHT-POINT PACT

A handsome man with crisp graying hair, Torrijos was the son of a school teacher. Born in 1929, he was trained for his career at the Military Academy of San Salvador, after which he joined Panama's National Guard and proved himself a brilliant officer. At the time he and several fellow officers overthrew President Arias and took control of Panama, he was a 39-year-old colonel. He and his colleagues moved against Arias because the president, long disliked by the Guard, was attempting to unseat some of its top officers.

To give the appearance of not violating Panama's constitution, which called for the country to be led by a president, Torrijos installed a close friend as president in Arias's place. But it was Torrijos who held the real power—the power of a dictator—in Panama.

Torrijos then sent representatives to seek a new Canal treaty.[3] They negotiated the matter with the administrations of three U.S. presidents—Richard Nixon, Gerald Ford, and Jimmy Carter. The negotiations bore their first fruit in 1974.

Signed that year was an agreement called the Eight-Point Pact. It was not a treaty in itself, but a document outlining the terms that the United States and Panama promised now to discuss for placement in a treaty. Among the eight terms due for discussion were: a higher annual Canal fee for Panama; the shared operation and defense of the waterway; and the promise that both nations would

General Omar Torrijos

work together in the future should the Canal need to be expanded.

The discussions that followed the announcement of the Eight-Point Pact lasted three years. They led to two treaties in 1977. President Jimmy Carter signed each for the United States, and General Torrijos signed for Panama. The signing took place on September 21, 1977.

THE FINAL STEP:
THE 1977 TREATIES

In the first of the two treaties, Panama and the United States pledged to keep the Canal neutral during any international or Panamanian disputes. The second pact concerned the future of the waterway and contained a variety of terms. We'll look at them now, taking each in turn.

A Change in Ownership
The most important of the terms was a startling one that went far beyond those mentioned for discussion in the Eight-Point Pact—and far beyond the terms of any treaty that the United States and Panama had ever before signed.

Surprising everyone, the United States agreed to give up its possession and control of the Canal on December 31, 1999. All U.S. administrators and military troops would withdraw from the Canal Zone by that date. Panama would be left in sole possession of the waterway—its outright owner and operator. The country would achieve the goal it had sought throughout the century. It would gain complete sovereignty over the stretch of land and the waterway that ran directly through its center.

As expected, the surrender of the Canal triggered a storm of protest throughout the United States. Countless Americans objected to giving away what they had always thought to be a national treasure. Many complained that the Canal would be ruined; the Panamanians would not have the expertise to run and maintain the waterway as well as the United States had.

Along with the protest, one question was asked everywhere: Why were the American negotiators willing to surrender such a national treasure? There were several possible answers.

For one, the U.S. was a troubled nation in the late 1970s. It was still recovering from the heartbreak and controversy caused by the Vietnam War. Also, the country was caught up in Middle Eastern disputes. It was clearly tired of its myriad problems. Further, President Carter looked on the Canal as a symbol of America's old reputation for butting into Latin American affairs. Many people, both in the United States and abroad, saw its surrender as America's way of solving one long-standing foreign problem and, at the same time, shedding itself of an old and unwanted reputation.

In addition, the waterway had once been of great military value to the United States because it enabled ships to move quickly from ocean to ocean. But that value had been reduced by modern air bombers and missiles. Also, missiles threatened attacks that would be difficult—if not impossible—to defend against and that could end the Canal's wartime value altogether.

Financially, the Canal may have been a national treasure, but it was no longer an economic one. It had been losing money since the early 1970s. While the costs of operation had risen through the years, the Canal tolls had been kept low to encourage its use. By 1973, this policy saw the Canal hit with a huge annual loss of $24 million. In that year, the tolls were raised for the first time in the Canal's history.

There was yet another economic reason. The waterway was approaching the day when it would be obsolete, no longer of use and no longer a moneymaker of any sort. It was becoming obsolete with the advent of "superships"— giant freighters and tankers—used in sea trade. These giant vessels were too big for the Canal to handle. They could not fit themselves into its 110-foot-wide (33.5 m) and 1,000-foot-long (340.8 m) locks.

In 1976, there were approximately 22,700 merchant vessels sailing the world's oceans. Of that number, some 1,300 were too large to pass through the Canal. Another 1,700 were so big that, when they were fully loaded, they rode too low in the water for the locks; on entering a lock, they would scrape along its bottom. In all, just over 12 percent of the world's merchant ships could not use the Canal. That percentage was sure to rise in the coming years.

As far back as the 1930s, the United States had been aware that larger and larger ships would be seen in the future. It had begun talking about increasing the size of the Canal locks to accommodate them. In 1939, it had launched a plan to construct larger locks, but World War II had put an end to the matter. There was more talk of larger locks during the post-war years, but the talk had died out by the early 1970s. By then, the United States was spending $30 million a year on the Vietnam War and Congress was in no mood to pour extra billions into a Canal project.

A Sea-Level Canal
The fact that the Canal was in danger of becoming obsolete was behind the next of the treaty's terms. The United States and Panama agreed to work together in studying the possibility of replacing the Canal with a sea-level waterway.[4]

Long before the idea of enlarging the locks came along, the U.S. had been talking about a sea-level canal.

In fact, talk in favor of a sea-level passage dated all the way back to 1903, when the decision to build a lock canal had been made. At that time, despite what had happened to de Lesseps, many U.S. leaders and engineers had favored a sea-level crossing and had said that America could succeed where the Frenchman had failed.

The idea for a sea-level canal hung on through the years. It was liked because it could be built to handle ships of the future which might be too big even for enlarged locks. It also promised to be less expensive to maintain and repair than a lock canal. And, of course, ships could travel its length more swiftly. They wouldn't have to enter any locks and wait for them to be filled.

By 1947, many engineers could see that the day of ships too large for the Canal was fast approaching. President Harry Truman received an engineering report that year. It urged the United States to prepare for the future by digging a sea-level passage. The new waterway would, the report said, follow a path near the Canal. But it would be five miles shorter and, as a result, would cut some four hours off the Isthmus crossing. The project was estimated to cost $2 billion.

Nothing was done about the idea, however, until the 1960s when President Lyndon B. Johnson's proposed treaty called for a study of a sea-level crossing. When the treaty negotiations collapsed, the matter was again shunted to the side—and remained there until it found a place in the 1977 treaty. By then, the estimated cost of building a sea-level passage had risen to $5 billion. But, despite the heavy cost, it was an idea worth studying, what with the Canal now on the verge of becoming obsolete.

The Passage of Ownership
The next term had to do with the Canal Zone and America's sovereignty there. Though Panama was not to take

possession of the Canal until the last day of 1999, America's sovereignty in the Zone was to end when the treaty took effect. The Zone itself was to be no more. The Panama Canal Company (which had operated and maintained the Canal) would be disbanded. Henceforth, the government and operation of the Canal would be in the hands of a nine-member group called the Panama Canal Commission.

The Commission would be composed of five Americans and four Panamanians. The United States held the right to appoint all the members, but the Panamanian government would be able to recommend the Panamanians to be appointed. The Commission's administrator—its chief officer—was to be an American until 1990. After that date, a Panamanian would serve as administrator. In addition to its regular duties, the Commission was charged with hiring an increasing number of Panamanians to work on the waterway as the years went by.

Other Principal Points
In addition to the points raised above, the treaty contained the following provisions:

> The United States and Panama were to cooperate in the defense of the Canal in times of war or Panamanian upheaval.

> The annual U.S. payment to Panama was to be upped to $10 million. An additional $10 million was to be paid annually to Panama from Canal revenues, plus a payment of 30 cents for each ton of shipping. These payments eventually added up to $80 million a year in the 1980s.

> On finally taking full possession of the Canal, Panama was free to employ Americans to help in its operation and maintenance.

President Jimmy Carter and Panamanian leader
Omar Torrijos sign the
Panama Canal treaty of 1977.

Once signed by Mr. Carter and General Torrijos, the treaties were approved by the Panamanian people in an election held in late 1977. Approval by the U.S. Senate came more slowly, with many of its members agreeing with the objections voiced by thousands of Americans to the loss of the Canal. Weeks of debate passed before the Senate ratified the treaties in 1978. They went into effect on October 1, 1979.

★ ★ ★

And so, the source of so many years of friction between Panama and the United States came to an end. The two countries entered a period of cooperation in the running of the Panama Canal—and a period of waiting for the day when the waterway will pass completely into Panamanian hands.

[9]
PANAMA AND THE
UNITED STATES TODAY

Despite the treaties of 1977, the 1980s have been marred by tensions between Panama and the United States. Unlike the troubles of earlier years, however, the tensions have not stemmed from problems over the Canal. At fault, rather, is the dictatorship that followed the Torrijos regime, which has been in power since 1984. The roots of this new dictatorship can be traced back to the mid-1970s.

A NEW DICTATORSHIP

By 1975, much of the Panamanian public had come to oppose Omar Torrijos, even though he had once been a very popular figure. [1] Many Panamanians disliked the General for exiling his political opponents and muzzling any newspaper that dared to criticize his rule. Many yearned for a nation of democratically elected presidents; Panama had not held a single open election since his rise to power; its presidents had been appointed by the National Assembly and had all been Torrijos's supporters. And there was deep concern over the way the General handled Panama's economy. The country was heavily in debt. The government was in danger of running out of money.

So great was the discontent that Torrijos finally said he would call for an open presidential election. Through no fault of his own, it was a vow he never kept. The General was killed in an airplane crash in 1981. For the next three years, Panama prepared itself for a presidential election.

The election—Panama's first in sixteen years—was held in May 1984.[2] After balloting that took days to count, candidate Nicolas Barletta was declared the winner. His opponent was the often-ousted Arnulfo Arias, now 83 years old. Barletta was backed by the National Guard, which had recently changed its name to the Panama Defense Forces (PDF).

A respected banker, Barletta promised to solve Panama's economic problems. But he failed to work fast enough to suit the Panama Defense Forces. In September 1984, he was ordered to resign by the PDF's commander, General Manuel Antonio Noriega. Barletta later said he had been kept a prisoner in his office by Noriega until he agreed to step down.

Noriega, who had commanded the PDF since 1983, replaced Barletta with Vice President Eric Delvalle. Everyone knew that the new president was merely a puppet leader and that Panama's first democratic election in sixteen years had done nothing but net the country a new dictator.

A HATED REGIME

Since taking over the nation, Noriega has been criticized by both the United States and great segments of the Panamanian public.[3]

General Manuel Antonio Noriega
*shortly after his opponent, former President
Eric Delvalle, went into hiding*

In 1986, on the basis of intelligence reports, the United States accused him of trafficking in drugs. The sources claimed that he was personally receiving millions of dollars from Latin American drug lords for allowing cocaine and marijuana to flow through Panama while en route to America and other nations. (The United States later indicted the General on drug charges and planned a trial on the matter. In 1989 the charges were upheld by a court in Miami, Florida.) The sources also revealed that he had sold arms to rebel troops who were attempting to overthrow the government of Colombia.

Finally, the sources accused Noriega of being involved in the murder of one of his chief political critics, Dr. Hugo Spadafora. Spadafora's body, tortured and beheaded, was found just over the border of neighboring Costa Rica in September 1985. The Noriega government held that he had been murdered in Costa Rica and that there was no evidence to connect the General to the crime. A later Costa Rican investigation concluded that Spadafora had been killed in Panama, after which his body had been dumped over the border.

The United States was not Panama's only neighbor to speak out against Noriega. Latin American nations such as Argentina, Brazil, Colombia, Mexico, Peru, Uruguay, and Venezuela also came to oppose his rule. They were joined by a number of European and Asian democracies.

Noriega's unpopularity inside Panama was based on many factors. People hated him for arresting his political enemies without good reason. Equally hated was his police force, whose members were known as the Dobermans, for the brutal way it treated anyone opposed to Noriega's regime. Also, many suspected that the General was guilty of fraud in the 1984 election by having his henchmen "stuff the ballot box" with votes for the PDF's candidate, Barletta.

And many suspected that Noriega had indeed taken part in the Spadafora murder. They pointed out that he had ousted Barletta from office just two weeks after the president announced he would form a commission to investigate Spadafora's death. Noriega's part in the murder, they charged, and not Barletta's failure to solve Panama's economic problems had been the real reason behind the ouster.

Angry at Noriega's alleged drug-trafficking involvement and concerned over the unrest in Panama, the administration of President Ronald Reagan attempted to unseat the dictator through a series of diplomatic moves. Between 1987 and early 1988, U.S. delegations visited Panama no fewer than eight times and urged Noriega to acknowledge his unpopularity and step down. The terms under which he might agree to do so were discussed. At one point in 1988, they seemed so personally favorable—and the opposition against him at home so strong—that he indicated a willingness to depart the country. In the end, however, he refused to leave and the talks came to nothing.

THE PEOPLE ACT

Panama's dislike of Noriega was clearly seen in late 1987. On October 9, some two thousand teachers marched in Panama City to demand improvements in the country's educational system; as they marched, they also chanted anti-Noriega slogans. A general strike and march was planned for October 22, but fell apart when more than one thousand soldiers dressed in battle gear were stationed along the route of the planned march. That day an electrical transmission tower was destroyed, cutting off electricity to most of Panama City.

By 1988, the opposition to Noriega was so strong that

President Delvalle decided he could be a puppet no longer.[4] Someone had to do something to ease the situation. And so, in March, he addressed the National Assembly and announced that he was asking Noriega to resign. Delvalle said that he wanted the General to step aside for the good of the country until the U.S. drug indictment against him was settled.

Within hours of the announcement, Noriega's supporters in the Assembly acted in the General's favor. They voted to dismiss Delvalle from the presidency and replace him with Manuel Palma, the nation's Minister of Education.

Delvalle refused to accept the Assembly's action and insisted that he was still president. Noriega immediately surrounded Delvalle's house with police, cut his telephone lines, and made him a virtual prisoner in his own home. Somehow, the beleaguered president managed to escape and went into hiding. In a later telephone conversation, he said that he had not left the country but was hidden somewhere in Panama. He vowed to fight on to hold the presidency.

Throughout the remainder of the 1980s an angry country waged a mounting campaign to unseat Noriega. It was a campaign that took many forms. For example, 1988 alone produced the following upheavals:

From early February to April, Panamanian workers staged a nationwide strike. Markets, department stores, restaurants, and factories were shut down. The country was paralyzed.

In March, a large anti-Noriega demonstration was staged outside a church in Panama City. The police moved in and used rubber clubs, birdshot, tear gas, and water cannon to break up the crowd.

> More than five thousand people marched along one
> of Panama City's main streets in April. They
> shouted the demand that Noriega resign. Again, the
> police moved in. While dragging marchers to waiting
> patrol wagons for the trip to jail, officers beat them
> with rubber clubs and rifle butts.

> Later that month, word came from Panama that the
> National Police Chief, Col. Leonidas Macias, and a
> number of fellow officers had tried to overthrow
> Noriega, but had failed. It was in great part because
> of this attempt that Noriega, during talks with visit-
> ing U.S. delegations, almost agreed to step down
> and depart Panama. The incident seemed to con-
> vince him of just how strongly he was opposed at
> home. Yet, in the end, he stubbornly chose to re-
> main.

In keeping with the Panamanian constitution, an election
to name a president for the country was held in 1989.[5]
Noriega put forward his own handpicked candidate,
Carlos Duque, for the post. The election campaign and
the election itself won international headlines. Here are
highlights of all that happened.

> The U.S. and Noriega's enemies at home accused
> him of trying to intimidate opposition candidates into
> not continuing their campaigns.

> When the election was held on May 8, the two
> major candidates—Noriega's Duque and the opposi-
> tion's Guillermo Endara—both claimed victory.
> Each based his claim on unofficial ballot counts.
> Foreign observers and leaders of Panama's Catholic
> church, on the basis of their own unofficial counts,

announced that Endara had won by a three-to-one margin. One foreign observer, former U.S. president Jimmy Carter, charged that the Noriega forces had made up false voter tally sheets in favor of their candidate. In Washington, D.C., President George Bush accused Noriega of election fraud.

When the unofficial counts gave strong indication that Endara had indeed defeated Noriega's Duque, government forces raided vote-counting centers and delayed the start of the official count. As a result, some 10,000 Panamanians staged demonstrations against Noriega.

On May 10, the Panamanian government declared the results of the election null and void. Noriega's representatives said that the election had been damaged by U.S. interference. The dictator remained in control of the country.

In late May, the Organization of American States (OAS), a body representing thirty-two Western Hemisphere nations, condemned Noriega for his political abuses, urged him to step down, and called for a "peaceful transfer" of power to a government elected by the people. Over the next months, OAS officials held talks with Noriega in the hopes of having him relinquish his hold on Panama. They had produced no results by the autumn of 1989.

Thousands of Panama's citizens march in protest against the pro-government party's claim of a victory in the 1988 national election.

NORIEGA AND THE CANAL

How did Panama's troubles affect the Canal?[6] There was concern that these problems would harm the waterway or its operations. However, all the demonstrations, marches, and riots stayed clear of the Canal and left it untouched. Clearly, the Panamanians understood its value to their country and had no intention of damaging it or its work.

A Plan Misfires

The Canal, however, played a part in the Noriega drama. In 1988 the dictator's opponents asked the United States to help restore peace in Panama by using military intervention to oust Noriega from power. The administration of President Ronald Reagan, angry at the general's alleged drug-trafficking activities, agreed to step in, but not through military action. Instead, the decision was made to starve Noriega with economic sanctions. The U.S. government banned its annual Canal payments to Panama, effectively cutting from Noriega revenues totaling $80 million a year. Later, Washington froze about $56 million in Panamanian assets that were banked in the United States. The freeze meant that they could not be used by Panama.

It was hoped that the ban and the freeze would produce such economic chaos that Noriega would be forced to resign in order to save his country from financial ruin. But the strategy misfired. Though both deeply wounded Panama's economy, Noriega stubbornly hung on.

Although the Canal was left in peace during the upheavals, the United States feared that harm might come to it at any time. In 1988 additional troops were sent to Panama to protect the waterway; 2,000 more were sent during the post-election upheavals. What were the threats feared by the United States? There was the danger that rioting in Panama City or Colón might accidentally spill over and touch the Canal. There was the chance that Noriega might close the waterway to American shipping, and the possibility that he might sabotage Canal operations and then attempt to discredit his opponents by blaming them. Not one of these fears became a reality.

However, the problems caused by the Noriega regime did have one adverse effect on one aspect of the 1977 treaties—the agreement to study the possibility of digging a sea-level waterway. In the early 1980s, the United States, Panama, and Japan agreed to study the feasibility of a sea-level canal. The trouble over Noriega caused the plans to be shunted aside indefinitely.

THE TENSIONS MOUNT

Following the 1989 election, the tensions increased between the United States and Noriega.[7] U.S. economic sanctions against the General's government continued, and the U.S. government pressed its demands to have Noriega brought to trial in Florida on drug charges.

On the other hand, the press reported Noriega's continuing accusations that the United States was interfering in Panamanian affairs. In October, a band of Panamanian soldiers and their officers made headlines when they attempted—but failed—to overthrow the dictator. The United States' alleged role in the action has never been clarified.

In December, the tensions between the two countries reached an intolerable level. Panama's chief legislative body, the National Assembly of Representatives (whose members had been appointed by Noriega) passed a resolution declaring the General to be the "maximum leader" of the nation. The resolution formally affirmed Noriega's absolute dictatorial powers. It stated that the reason for his appointment was American "aggression," a reference to the economic sanctions of the past months and Noriega's growing fear that the U.S. might embark on a military action in the Isthmus. Noriega declared the two countries to be in a "state of war."

One day later, a U.S. soldier was shot and killed by Panamanian soldiers when his car was stopped at a checkpoint in Panama City. Noriega's government claimed that the soldier had died after he and his four companions opened fire on the Panamanian troops at the checkpoint. The United States vehemently denied the charge.

Though there had been earlier reports of Americans being harassed by Noriega's forces, the December incident marked the first time that an American had died at Panamanian hands. The administration of recently elected President George Bush declared that an end had to be put to Noriega's regime and that he had to be captured and brought to the U.S. for trial on long-standing drug charges.

Consequently, some 24,000 American troops attacked Panama on December 20. Several days of intense fighting against soldiers and citizens loyal to the dictator followed. As the invading troops took control of Panama City, the United States recognized Guillermo Endara—who had claimed victory in the May election—as the legitimate president of the nation. Endara quickly began to assemble a new government. The General went into hiding.

Noriega eluded capture until Christmas Eve. That day, he suddenly appeared at the Vatican embassy in Panama City to request—and be granted—political sanctuary there. As is true of all embassies, the Vatican facility is considered immune from intrusion by outsiders, and so U.S. troops could not enter it and take him captive.

The U.S. invasion was met with both applause and condemnation. Supporters held that the Bush administration had taken a long-overdue step in toppling a man they believed was a vicious dictator and drug dealer. But a number of Latin nations—Cuba and Colombia among them—accused Mr. Bush of using "bully" tactics. They charged that, by assaulting such a small country, the United States was again using military might to force its will on countries south of its borders.

(Above) Anti-Noriega demonstrators crowd around a
blockade of U.S. Army
armored vehicles parked on
an avenue leading to the
Vatican Embassy, where former
Panamanian dictator Manuel
Noriega had sought refuge.

(Left) Noriega poses for a
booking mugshot after he
surrendered to U.S. military
authorities on January 3, 1990.

Once Noriega entered the Vatican embassy, many questions arose concerning his future. Would he be allowed to remain in sanctuary there for an indefinite period of time? Would he be exiled to another country? Would negotiations that began between the embassy and the United States see him turned over to American authorities? Or would negotiations between the embassy and the new Endara government see him handed over to the Panamanians?

On January 3, 1990, Noriega himself supplied the answers. He left the embassy and surrendered to American authorities. The press reported that his surrender was prompted in great part by two fears: first, that he would be harmed by the Isthmus people if the embassy released him into their hands and, second, that his life would be in constant danger from angry Panamanians were he sent into exile in another country.

As public celebrations erupted in Panama and as the United States began to plan to send the first of its troops home, the General was flown to Miami, Florida, to be arraigned on January 4 on drug charges. As this book is being completed, Manuel Noriega's power is at an end in Panama and he is awaiting trial for his drug-trafficking activities.

And so, Panama and the United States are entering the decade that will see the Panama Canal transferred from one to the other. Will the fall of General Noriega signal the beginning of new and cordial relations between the two countries? Or will they encounter new troubles? We can only hope that the former proves to be true. For then we can hope that, by the time the Canal passes into Panamanian hands, the two nations will have put their old problems far behind them. They can embark on a new century not as troubled neighbors but as good friends.

SOURCE NOTES

CHAPTER ONE
THE BRIDGE OF LAND

1. The material on Christopher Columbus and his first three voyages to the New World is developed from: T. A. Bailey, *The American Pageant: A History of the Republic* (Boston: D. C. Heath, 1956), 7; M. Burke, *United States History: The Growth of Our Land* (Chicago: American Technical Society, 1957), 5–6; J. D. Hicks, *The Federal Union: A History of the United States to 1865* (Boston: Houghton Mifflin, 1952), 11; E. F. Tschan, H. J. Grimm, J. D. Squires, *Western Civilization: The Decline of Rome to 1660* (New York: J. B. Lippincott, 1942), 546–47.

2. The material on the fourth voyage of Columbus is developed from: V. Stefansson, *Great Adventures and Explorations* (New York: Dial Press, 1947), 219–20.

3. The material on Panama's name and location is developed from: H. H. Barrows, E. P. Parker, C. W. Sorensen, *The American Continents* (Morristown, N.J.: Silver Burdett, 1961), 307; *The World: Its Geography in Maps* (Chicago: Denoyer-Geppert, 1962), 58–59.

4. The material on the geography, population, and economy of Panama is developed from: Barrows, Parker, and Sorensen, 307; R. F. Nyrop, editor, *Panama: A Country Study* (Washington, D.C.: U.S. Government, 1980), xiii–xv, 5, 54–59, 89–129; "Delvalle Freezes Assets Abroad," *Facts on File*, March 4, 1988, 137; *The 1989 Information Please Almanac* (Boston: Houghton Mifflin, 1989), 241.

5. The introductory material on the Panama Canal is developed from: D. McCullough, *The Path Between the Seas: The Creation of the Panama Canal, 1870–1914* (New York: Simon and Schuster, 1977), 34; Nyrop, 3; S. Winchester, "Panama: Canal 'In Jeopardy,'" *World Press Review,* April 1988, 11; *The 1989 Information Please Almanac,* 241–242; "U.S. Withholds Canal Payments," *Facts on File,* March 18, 1988, 181.

CHAPTER TWO
THE MAGNIFICENT DREAM

1. R. F. Nyrop, editor, *Panama: A Country Study* (Washington, D.C.: U.S. Government, 1980), 6.

2. The material on Balboa's early life, his stay at Hispaniola, his voyage with Enciso, and his supervision of the Santa Maria settlement is developed from: Nyrop, 6; P. Rink, *The Land Divided, The World United: The Story of the Panama Canal* (New York: Julian Messner, 1963), 28; V. Stefansson, *Great Adventures and Explorations* (New York: Dial Press, 1947), 225–26, 228–29.

3. The material on Balboa's journey to the Pacific Ocean is developed from: B. Considine, *The Panama Canal* (New York: Random House, 1951), 10–12; Nyrop, 6–7; C. O. Sauer, *The Early Spanish Main* (Berkeley: University of California Press, 1966), 231–37; Stefansson, 227, 228, 229–31.

4. The material on Panama's growth and importance as a Spanish holding is developed from: Nyrop, 9–10.

5. The material on the early land trails across the Panamanian Isthmus is developed from: Rink, 29, 30–31, 36, 37, 42, 48.

6. M. Burke, *United States History: The Growth of Our Land* (Chicago: American Technical Society, 1957), 9; Nyrop, 7.

7. The material on the early dreams of a trans-Panamanian waterway is developed from: D. McCullough, *The Path Between the Seas: The Creation of the Panama Canal, 1870–1914* (New York: Simon and Schuster, 1977), 27; Rink, 29, 30–31.

CHAPTER THREE
A NEW AND
GROWING INTEREST

1. The material on Alexander von Humboldt and the international interest created by his writings on possible Panama canal routes is developed

from: B. Considine, *The Panama Canal* (New York: Random House, 1951), 19–22; E. F. Dolan, *Green Universe: The Story of Alexander von Humboldt* (New York: Dodd, Mead, 1958), 177; D. McCullough, *The Path Between the Seas: The Creation of the Panama Canal, 1870–1914* (New York: Simon and Schuster, 1977), 28–30.

2. The material on Spain's loss of its South American and Mexican holdings and the effects of the Spanish loss of Colombia on Panama is developed from: W. L. Neff and M. G. Planer, *World History for a Better World* (Milwaukee, Wis.: Bruce Publishing, 1958), 517–18, 519, 521; R. F. Nyrop, editor, *Panama: A Country Study* (Washington, D.C.: U.S. Government, 1980), 14–15; P. Rink, *The Land Divided, The World United: The Story of the Panama Canal* (New York: Julian Messner, 1963), 43. *The Concord Desk Encyclopedia* (New York: Concord Reference Books, 1982), Vol. 1, 176, 273, 302, Vol. 2, 801–02, 861, Vol. 3, 1244.

3. The material on the Central American Federation and its canal dealings with the United States and Holland is developed from: Rink, 44–45.

4. The material on the Monroe Doctrine and the foreign reactions to it is developed from: T. A. Bailey, *The American Pageant: A History of the Republic* (Boston: D. C. Heath, 1956), 239–240; M. Burke, *United States History: The Growth of Our Land* (Chicago: American Technical Society, 1957), 93–94; Considine, 23, 27–28, 36.

5. The material on the developments between 1846 and 1850 (the Bidlack Treaty, the Panama route to the American West, and the construction of the Panama Railroad) that increased United States interest in a Panamanian canal is developed from: Considine, 25–28; McCullough, 33, 35, 38; Nyrop, 16, 18, 19.

6. The material on the Clayton-Bulwer Treaty is developed from: Bailey, 387; Burke, 147; Considine, 47; McCullough, 38.

CHAPTER FOUR
AMERICA TAKES OVER

1. The material on the French determination to build a Panamanian canal is developed from: B. Considine, *The Panama Canal* (New York, Random House, 1951), 42; P. Rink, *The Land Divided, The World United: The Story of the Panama Canal* (New York: Julian Messner, 1963), 65.

2. Rink, 61–62.

3. The material on the French effort to build the Panama Canal is developed from: Considine, 45–47, 56, 60–63, 65–66; S. E. Morison and

H. S. Commager, *The Growth of the American Republic, 1865–1950* (New York: Oxford University Press, 1950), 402; R. F. Nyrop, editor, *Panama: A Country Study* (Washington, D.C.: U. S. Government, 1980), 19–20, 22, 26; Rink, 75–77.

4. The material on America's growing interest in building the Panama Canal and the developments (the Spanish-American War, the French offer to sell its Canal rights, the Hay-Pauncefote Treaty, and the Hay-Herran Treaty) that led to the U.S. construction of the waterway is developed from: Considine, 72–74; J. D. Hicks, *A Short History of American Democracy* (Boston: Houghton Mifflin, 1949), 603, 606, 625–26; S. E. Morison and Commager, 401–403; Nyrop, 22; Rink, 82–84.

5. The material on Panama's successful bid for independence as a nation is developed from: Considine, 77–79; D. McCullough, *The Path Between the Seas: The Creation of the Panama Canal, 1870–1914* (New York: Simon and Schuster, 1977), 364, 366–67; Morison and Commager, 403–04; Rink, 85–90.

CHAPTER FIVE
A CANAL IS BUILT

1. The material on the Hay–Bunau-Varilla Treaty is developed from: J. D. Hicks, *A Short History of American Democracy* (Boston: Houghton Mifflin, 1949), 626; D. McCullough, *The Path Between the Seas: The Creation of the Panama Canal, 1870–1914* (New York: Simon and Schuster, 1977), 392–93; R. F. Nyrop, editor, *Panama: A Country Study* (Washington, D.C.: U.S. Government, 1980), 23–24; P. Rink, *The Land Divided, The World United: The Story of the Panama Canal* (New York: Julian Messner, 1963), 91.

2. The description of the Panama Canal and the account of a journey through it are developed from: B. Considine, *The Panama Canal* (New York: Random House, 1951), 150–53, 167–70; McCullough, 165, 195, 307, 308, 484, 488–89, 539–40, 590–604, map following 465; Nyrop, 165; Rink, 13–16, 123, 127, 132, 137–8; *The Panama Canal*, an informational brochure (Panama: Panama Canal Office of Public Affairs, November 1985), no page number given.

3. The material on the preparations for the construction of the Canal is developed from: Considine, 96, 98, 103–05, 122–23, 126.

4. The material on the medical work of William Crawford Gorgas is developed from: E. F. Dolan, *Walter Reed: Vanquishing Yellow Fever* (Chicago: Britannica Books, 1962), 189; Dolan and H. T. Silver, *William*

Crawford Gorgas: Warrior in White (New York: Dodd, Mead, 1968), 124–25, 129, 141, 196–97, 201–02; Nyrop, 26.

5. The material on the construction of the Panama Canal is developed from: Considine, 134–38; 143–147; McCullough, 543–54, 581, 589–94, 601; Rink, 129–30, 137–40, 143–50.

CHAPTER SIX
AN ANGRY PANAMA

1. The material on the tonnage and cargoes shipped through the Panama Canal—and the tolls charged—since its opening is developed from: B. Considine, *The Panama Canal* (New York: Random House, 1951), 171; R. F. Nyrop, editor, *Panama: A Country Study* (Washington, D.C.: U.S. Government, 1980), 94–95, 124–25, 127; P. Rink, *The Land Divided, The World United: The Story of the Panama Canal* (New York: Julian Messner, 1963), 173, 175; "Delvalle Freezes Assets Abroad," *Facts on File*, March 4, 1988, 137.

2. The material on the benefits derived from the Canal by the Panamanian people is developed from: Nyrop, 94, 162; Rink, 175.

3. The material on the discontent caused the Panamanian people by the Canal is developed from: D. McCullough, *The Path Between the Seas: The Creation of the Panama Canal, 1870–1914* (New York: Simon and Schuster, 1977), 147, 161–62, 471–72; Nyrop, 23, 27, 94, 153, 161, 168; Rink, 81, 91, 175–76.

CHAPTER SEVEN
RIGHTING THE WRONGS

1. The material on United States intervention in Panamanian affairs is developed from: R. F. Nyrop, editor, *Panama: A Country Study* (Washington, D.C.: U.S. Government, 1980), 27–28.

2. The material on United States discriminatory practices in the Canal Zone and U.S. views of the Canal as a personal possession is developed from: D. McCullough, *The Path Between the Seas: The Creation of the Panama Canal, 1870–1914* (New York: Simon and Schuster, 1951), 472; Nyrop, 29–30.

3. The material on the first Panamanian constitution is developed from: Nyrop, 24, 134.

4. The material on America's growing dislike of its interventionist policies and the resultant emergence of President Franklin Roosevelt's "Good

Neighbor Policy" is developed from: T. A. Bailey, *The American Pageant: A History of the Republic* (Boston: D. C. Heath, 1956), 698, 830, 859–60; M. Burke, *United States History: The Growth of Our Land* (Chicago: American Technical Society, 1957), 151; J. D. Hicks, *A Short History of American Democracy* (Boston: Houghton Mifflin, 1949), 831–32; S. E. Morison and H. S. Commager, *The Growth of the American Republic, 1865–1950* (New York: Oxford University Press, 1950), 405–07; W. E. Neff and M. G. Planer, *World History for a Better World* (Milwaukee, Wis.: Bruce Publishing, 1958), 679–80; Nyrop, 28.

5. The material on the Hull-Alfaro Treaty is developed from: Nyrop, 29–31.

6. The material on the events leading to World War II and then the emergence of the National Guard in postwar Panamanian affairs is developed from: Hicks, 835–36; Nyrop, 31–33.

7. The material on the Eisenhower-Remon Treaty is developed from: Nyrop, 34.

CHAPTER EIGHT
THE FINAL STEPS

1. The material on the events leading to the flying of the Panamanian flag in the Canal Zone is developed from: R. F. Nyrop, editor, *Panama: A Country Study* (Washington, D.C.: U.S. Government, 1980), 35, 37–38.

2. The material on the negotiations by Panamanian leaders Chiari, Robles, and Torrijos that led to the signing of the 1977 Canal Treaties is developed from: Nyrop, 38–39, 44–45, 46–48, 126–29; "Torrijos Killed in Air Crash," *Facts on File*, August 7, 1981, 564; "Post-Torrijos Power Struggle Seen," *Facts on File*, December 31, 1981, 994.

3. The material on the 1977 Canal treaties is developed from: Nyrop, 48–49, 196–97; "Carter, Torrijos Sign New Panama Canal Treaties: Latin American Presidents Attend OAS Ceremony," *Facts on File*, September 10, 1977, 677; "Text of Treaties Signed by U.S. and Panama," *Facts on File*, September 10, 1977, 679–82; "Panama Canal," *Facts on File*, September 17, 1977.

4. The material on a possible sea-level waterway to replace the present Canal is developed from: B. Considine, *The Panama Canal* (New York: Random House, 1951), 176–78; Nyrop, 46, 231–32, 236, 238; P. Rink, *The Land Divided, The World United: The Story of the Panama Canal* (New York: Julian Messner, 1963), 178; "New Latin Route Proposed," *Facts on File*, September 25/October 1, 1969, 625.

CHAPTER NINE
PANAMA AND THE
UNITED STATES TODAY

1. The material on the final years of the Torrijos regime is developed from: R. F. Nyrop, editor, *Panama: A Country Study* (Washington, D.C.: U.S. Government, 1980), 151–52.

2. The material on the Barletta presidency is developed from: "Close Election Raises Tension," *Facts on File*, May 11, 1984, 344; "Ardito Barletta Declared President," *Facts on File*, May 18, 1984, 359; "Ardito Barletta Sworn President," *Facts on File*, October 12, 1984, 758; "Military Ousts Barletta," *Facts on File*, October 4, 1985, 744–75.

3. The material on Manuel Noriega, the accusations of his drug trafficking, his alleged involvement in the Spadafora killing, and the U.S. attempts to negotiate his departure from Panama is developed from: J. Greenwald, "Panama: Kiss, Kiss, Bang, Bang," *Time*, March 28, 1988, 32–33; T. Morganthau, "Anatomy of a Fiasco," *Newsweek*, June 6, 1988, 36; G. Mott, "Noriega: The Long Goodbye," *Newsweek*, May 9, 1988, 32; C. A. Robbins, "The Noriega Saga: The Next Chapter," *U.S. News & World Report*, May 2, 1988, 44; J. Smoleve, "The Drug Thugs," *Time*, March 7, 1988, 30, 31; S. Winchester, "Panama: Canal 'In Jeopardy,' " *World Press Review*, April, 1988, 11; "Military Critic Found Slain," *Facts on File*, October 4, 1985, 745; "U.S. Ties Military Chief to Drugs, Murder," *Facts on File*, June 20, 1986, 456; "Spadafora Murder," *Facts on File*, June 20, 1986, 457; "Panamanian Military Leader Named in U.S. Drug Charges," *Facts on File*, February 12, 1988, 78–79; "Panama Faces Cash Crisis," *Facts on File*, March 11, 1988, 158; "Noriega Charge Upheld in U.S.," *Facts on File*, January 20, 1989, 39; "The Bait-and-Switch Artist Strikes Again," *U.S. News & World Report*, May 23, 1988, 25.

4. The material on Delvalle's failed attempt to unseat Noriega and the resultant actions by angry Panamanians and the U.S. government is developed from: J. Greenwald, "Still in Charge," *Time*, March 7, 1988, 26–27; Morganthau, 36–37; C. A. Robbins, "Waiting for the Next Coup to Topple Noriega," *U.S. News & World Report*, April 25, 1988, 36; "Panama's President Ousted: Move to Fire Noriega Failed," *Facts on File*, March 4, 1988, 137–138.

5. The material on the 1989 Panamanian presidential election is developed from: L. Gruson, "Referendum on Noriega Splits Voters," *New York Times*, May 7, 1989; "Panama Election Voided Amid Charges of Government Fraud, Foreign Intervention," *Facts on File*, May 12, 1989, 347–48; "OAS Condemns Panama's Noriega," *Facts on File*, May 19, 1989, 356;

"U.S. Says Noriega Rigging Elections," *San Francisco Chronicle,* April 21, 1989; "Heavy Vote In Panama—Noriega Under Fire," *San Francisco Chronicle* (from a *Washington Post* report), May 8, 1989; "Carter Says Noriega Stealing the Election," *San Francisco Chronicle,* May 9, 1989; "Panama Crisis Confounds OAS," *San Francisco Chronicle* (an Associated Press report), May 27, 1989; "Noriega Refuses to Budge—OAS Mission Called 'Disaster,' " *San Francisco Chronicle* (from a *New York Times* report), June 20, 1989.

6. The material on the effects of the Noriega situation on the Panama Canal is developed from: A. Bilski, "Noriega's Tightening Grip," *Maclean's,* April 11, 1988, 17; J. Greenwald, "Panama: Kiss, Kiss, Bang, Bang," *Time,* March 28, 1988; S. Winchester, "Panama: Canal 'In Jeopardy,' " *World Press Review,* April 1988, 11; "U.S. Rules Out Military Intervention," *Facts on File,* March 4, 1988, 137; "U.S. Withholds Canal Payments," *Facts on File,* March 18, 1988, 181; "U.S. Officials Allege Harassment at the Canal," *San Francisco Chronicle* (from a *New York Times* report), May 19, 1989.

7. The material on the mounting Noriega-U.S. tensions, the American attack on Panama, Noriega's sanctuary in the Vatican embassy, and his final surrender to U.S. authorities is developed from: W. Branigin, "Noriega Declared 'Maximum Leader' of Panama," *Washington Post,* December 16, 1989; "U.S. Soldier Slain Near Noriega HQ," *San Francisco Examiner* (from Associated Press), December 17, 1989; "Bush Accuses Noriega of Harassing GIs," *San Francisco Chronicle* (from *Washington Post*), December 18, 1989; "U.S. Attacks Noriega Stronghold," *San Francisco Chronicle,* December 20, 1989; J. Gerstenzang and J. Nelson, "U.S. Presses to Get Noriega Out for Trial," *San Francisco Chronicle* (from *Los Angeles Times*), December 26, 1989; "Noriega Surrenders to U.S.: Former Dictator Faces Drug Trial," *San Francisco Chronicle* (from *New York Times* and Chronicle Wire Service), January 4, 1990; G. J. Church, "No Place to Run," *Time,* January 8, 1990, 38–42.

[★]
BIBLIOGRAPHY

BOOKS

Bailey, Thomas A. *The American Pageant: A History of the Republic.* Boston: D.C. Heath, 1956.

Barrows, Harlan H.; Parker, Edith Putnam; and Sorensen, Clarence W. *The American Continents.* Morristown, N.J.: Silver Burdett, 1961.

Biesanz, John and Mavis. *The People of Panama.* New York: Columbia University Press, 1955.

Burke, Merle. *United States History: The Growth of Our Land.* Chicago: American Technical Society, 1957.

Chidsey, Donald Barr. *The Panama Canal: An Informal History.* New York: Crown, 1970.

Considine, Bob. *The Panama Canal.* New York: Random House, 1951.

Dolan, Edward F. *Green Universe: The Story of Alexander von Humboldt.* New York: Dodd, Mead, 1959.

_____ *Walter Reed: Vanquishing Yellow Fever.* Chicago: Britannica Books, 1962.

_____ *The Explorers: Adventures in Courage.* Chicago: Reilly & Lee, 1970.

Dolan, Edward F. and Silver, H.T. *William Crawford Gorgas: Warrior in White.* New York: Dodd, Mead, 1968.

Dubois, Jules. *Danger Over Panama.* Indianapolis: Bobbs-Merrill, 1964.

Duval, Miles, P., Jr. *And the Mountains Will Move: The Story of the Building of the Panama Canal.* Stanford and Palo Alto, Calif.: Stanford University Press, 1947.

Fast, Howard. *Goethals and the Panama Canal.* New York: Julian Messner, 1942.

Herring, Hubert. *A History of Latin America.* 3rd ed., rev. New York: Knopf, 1968.

Howarth, David. *Panama: Four Hundred Years of Dreams and Cruelty.* New York: McGraw-Hill, 1966.

LaFeber, Walter. *The Panama Canal: The Crisis in Historical Perspective.* New York: Oxford University Press, 1979.

McCullough, David. *The Path Between the Seas: The Creation of the Panama Canal, 1870–1914.* New York: Simon & Schuster, 1977.

Morison, Samuel Eliot and Commager, Henry Steele. *The Growth of the American Republic, 1865–1950.* New York: Oxford University Press, 1950.

Neff, William Lee and Planer, Mabel Gertrude. *World History for a Better World.* Milwaukee, Wis.: Bruce Publishing, 1958.

Nyrop, Richard F. *Panama: A Country Study.* Washington, D.C.: American University, Foreign Area Studies, 1980. (Copyright, United States Government as represented by the Secretary of the Army.)

Rink, Paul. *The Land Divided, The World United: The Story of the Panama Canal.* New York: Julian Messner, 1963.

MAGAZINES

Armbrister, Trevor. "Panama: Why They Hate Us," *The Saturday Evening Post,* March 7, 1964.

Billard, Jules B. "Panama, Link Between Oceans and Continents," *National Geographic,* March 1970.

Bilski, Andrew. "Noriega's Tightening Grip," *Maclean's,* April 11, 1988.

Facts on File. "Reagan Meets Panamanian President," October 22, 1982.

——— "Latin America," January 21, 1983.

——— "Panama Canal: Declining Traffic, Toll Revenues Seen," February 18, 1983.

——— "Panama: National Guard Chief Resigns," August 19, 1983.

——— "Panama: Close Election Raises Tension," May 11, 1984.

——— "Panama: Ardito Barletta Declared President," May 18, 1984.

——— "Panama: Ardito Barletta Sworn President," October 12, 1984.

——— "Panama: Military Ousts President," October 4, 1985.

——— "Barletta Ousted; Failed to Solve Panama's Economic Problems," April 18, 1986.

——— "Panama: Vice President's Office Closed," November 18, 1987.

——— "Panama: Noriega Foe Sentenced," December 31, 1987.

_____ "Panamanian Military Leader Named in U.S. Drug Charges,"
February 12, 1988.
_____ "Panama's President Ousted; Move to Fire Noriega Failed,"
March 4, 1988.
_____ "Panama Faces Cash Crisis," March 11, 1988.
_____ "U.S. Withholds Canal Payments," March 18, 1988.
_____ "U.S. Troops Sent to Panama to Protect Military Bases," April
8, 1988.
_____ "Panama: 'State of Urgency' Declared," June 12, 1988.
_____ "Panama: U.S. Ties Army Chief to Drugs, Murder," June 20,
1988.
_____ "Panama Election Voided Amid Charges of Government Fraud,
Foreign Intervention," May 12, 1989.
Galloway, Joseph L., with Lief, Louise; Borger, Gloria; and Kaylor, Robert.
"Post Mortem on the Rout in Panama," *U.S. News & World Report,*
June 6, 1988.
Geyelin, Philip. "The Irksome Panama Wrangle," *The Reporter,* April 9,
1964.
Greenwald, John. "Still in Charge: An Attempt to Oust Panama's Boss
Highlights a Hemispheric Crisis," *Time,* March 7, 1988.
_____ "Panama: Kiss, Kiss, Bang, Bang," *Time,* March 28, 1988.
Langley, L.D. "U.S.-Panamanian Relations Since 1941," *Journal of Inter-
American Studies,* July 1970.
Morganthau, Tom, with Waller, Douglas, and Lane, Charles. "Anatomy of
a Fiasco," *Newsweek,* June 6, 1988.
Mott, Gordon, with Gonzalez, David L., and Waller, Douglas, "Impa-
tience Over Panama: Narrowing U.S. Options," *Newsweek,* April 11,
1988.
Mott, Gordon, with Waller, Douglas, and Lane, Charles. "Noriega: The
Long Goodbye," *Newsweek,* May 9, 1988.
Needler, Martin C. "Omar Torrijos: The Panamanian Enigma," *Intellect,*
February 1977.
Robbins, Carla Anne. "Waiting for the Next Coup to Topple Noriega,"
U.S. News & World Report, April 25, 1988.
_____ "Central America: The Grand Botch," *U.S. News & World
Report,* June 6, 1988.
Robbins, Carla Anne, with Chesnoff, Richard Z., and Rosenthal, James.
"The Noriega Saga: Next Chapter," *U.S. News & World Report,* May
2, 1988.
Rosenfeld, Stephen J. "The Panama Negotiations: A Close-Run Thing,"
Foreign Affairs, October 1975.
U.S. News & World Report. "Now it's a Two-Way Squeeze," April 18,
1988.

Winchester, Simon. "Panama: Canal in Jeopardy," *World Press Review*, April 1988.

NEWSPAPERS

New York Times. "Deposed Panama President Offers to Give Up His Claim," October 10, 1988.

San Francisco Chronicle, "U.S. Attack in Panama 'Imminent,' " July 2, 1988.

──────── "Panama Giving Cold Shoulder to Agency That Runs the Canal" (from *New York Times*), July 13, 1988.

──────── "Noriega Warns U.S. Against Breaking Panama Canal Treaty" (from *Washington Post*), August 13, 1988.

──────── "Panama President Assails U.S. Before U.N. General Assembly" (from Reuters), September 28, 1988.

──────── "U.S. Marines Confront Intruders at Air Base," October 2, 1988.

──────── "U.S. Suspected Noriega 15 Years Ago" (from United Press International), October 6, 1988.

──────── "U.S. Says Noriega Rigging Election," April 21, 1989.

──────── "Heavy Vote in Panama—Noriega Under Fire" (from *Washington Post*), May 8, 1989.

──────── "Carter Says Noriega Stealing the Election," May 9, 1989.

──────── "Panama Crisis Confounds OAS" (from Associated Press), May 27, 1989.

──────── "Noriega Refuses to Budge—OAS Mission Called 'Disaster' " (from *New York Times*), June 20, 1989.

──────── "U.S. Officials Allege Harassment at the Canal" (from *New York Times*), May 19, 1989.

San Francisco Examiner. "The Other Panama," February 22, 1987.

[★]
INDEX